BY ANY
OTHER NAME

■

BY ANY OTHER NAME

■

Michael D. Shook

Prentice Hall General Reference

New York   London   Toronto   Sydney   Tokyo   Singapore

PRENTICE HALL GENERAL REFERENCE
15 Columbus Circle
New York, New York, 10023

PRENTICE HALL is a registered trademark and
colophon is a trademark of Prentice-Hall, Inc.

Contact Library of Congress for full CIP data.

ISBN 0-671-86475-0

Designed by Rhea Braunstein

Manufactured in the United States of America

10 9 8 7 6 5 4 3 2 1

First Edition

For my father, Robert L. Shook.

ACKNOWLEDGMENTS

I am grateful to the following people who helped me in some way with the researching and preparation of this book: Jarred Coopersmith, John Distefano, Sarah Hamilton, Mary Liff, Carrie Shook, R. J. Shook, and most important my father, Robert L. Shook, who is a professional writer (as is my sister, Carrie).

And special thank yous to my agent, Jeff Herman, and my editor, Deirdre Mullane.

I am sorry if I inadvertently left out any names; it is possible that my mind was preoccupied with the assembling of the thousands of other names that appear in this book.

CONTENTS

Introduction	xi
How Some Familiar Things Were Named	1
Proper Names That Became Words	21
The Most Common Names in America	39
Our Fifty States	47
State Nicknames	55
How Some American Cities Were Named	63
City Nicknames	79
Unusual Place Names	89
Presidential Nicknames	109
Native American Tribal Names	117
Stage Names, Pen Names, and Other Famous Pseudonyms	125
Nicknames of College Teams	149
The Name of the Game Is Sports	179
Corporate Names	211
Trademark Names	235
Colorful Names on Wall Street	251
Comic Strip Characters	261

INTRODUCTION

"What's in a name? That which we call a rose
By any other name would smell as sweet."
William Shakespeare
Romeo and Juliet, act 2, scene 1

You name it—everyone and everything has one. What makes it all so interesting is how people, places, and things got their names. As you will discover, some names resulted from considerable thought, while others came about in a more casual fashion.

In 1972, for example, after having been in business for 90 years, Standard Oil Company made a major effort to change its name. To do so, the giant oil company spent $100 million, making it the most expensive name change ever. The conversion involved an extensive study of more than 100 languages, more than 7,000 interviews, and the examination of more than 15,000 telephone books. Three years later, when the great name search was over, the new name was announced: *Exxon.* Why Exxon? Linguistic consultants wanted a name that had no actual meaning in *any* language. They wanted to make sure the name didn't offend anyone anywhere in the world or wouldn't infringe on an existing trademark. By creating a brand-new word that nobody had ever heard, the company was able to avoid any confrontations. *Exxon* was also an easy word to pronounce in most languages and it was a memorable word: The double "x" was thought to be a distinctive design—it had what the experts called "eye appeal."

Imagine all the stationery, oil cans, and road maps with

Standard Oil printed on them that had to be relabeled. Then there were the thousands of service stations that had to have their signs changed, the billboards on the highways, and so on. All in all, it was a tremendous effort.

While some names are chosen deliberately and with much fanfare, as with Exxon's, others come about almost by accident. Such is the case with the naming of South America and North America. While searching for a shorter route to the Far East in 1492, Christopher Columbus believed that he had landed at his destination. So he called the natives Indians, thinking he was in the Indies. However, it was Amerigo Vespucci (1454–1512), a rather obscure navigator, who figured out that Columbus was mistaken. As a reward for declaring that Columbus discovered two new continents, Amerigo Vespucci was immortalized forever as the man for whom the two great continents in the Western Hemisphere were named.

Of course, a lot of things are named for the people who first discovered or invented them. John Montagu, the fourth earl of Sandwich, for instance, liked to put a slice of meat between two pieces of bread; as a result, the word *sandwich* has become a permanent word in our vocabulary. Then there was Louis XV's beautiful mistress, Madame de Pompadour, who wore her lovely golden hair swept straight up from the forehead, after whom the word *pompadour* has become a part of our language. Union General Joseph Hooker of Civil War fame had a particular fondness for prostitutes, who since then have also been referred to as *hookers*. As you read *By Any Other Name*, you'll meet all sorts of interesting people whose names are household words such as *maverick, boycott, cardigan,* and *derringer*.

You will learn how our 50 states were named and how many of our cities and states got their nicknames (did you know that Chicago is an Indian word for "place where the wild onions grow"?). Iowa, for instance, is known as the *Hawkeye State* in reference to an Indian chief by the same name. And Chicago is called the *Windy City,* not because of its weather and ferocious wind velocity, but instead due to its long-winded politicians.

In other chapters, you will learn the stories behind some of the most well-known U.S. trademarks including Coca Cola, Xerox and Aunt Jemima. You'll find out how well-established trademarks were lost and became generic words—including *aspirin, linoleum, shredded wheat,* and *yo-yo.* And if you're a sports fan, there are chapters devoted to how teams and athletes got their colorful nicknames.

There's much more, including nicknames of U.S. presidents, what Indian tribal names mean, and how some of the most bizarre and zany names were given to places across our great land.

So read on for an informative and entertaining look at how some of the most common people, places, and things were named.

How Some Familiar Things Were Named

■

Did you ever think about why it's called a *funny bone* or a *kangaroo court?* Or why we keep *minutes* at a meeting? And why we refer to a football field as a *gridiron,* or a golf course as the *links?* This chapter will tell you how all of these things got named and a whole lot more.

Why is the American dollar called a *buck?* American fur traders classified skins as *bucks* and *does.* Bucks, being larger, were worth more. By 1850, the term *buck,* meaning a dollar, had come into wide use.

Why is a ten-dollar bill called a *sawbuck?* A *sawbuck* has been a slang term for a ten-dollar bill since before 1850. A sawbuck was originally a sawhorse with the legs projecting above the crossbar forming an X at each end. Since an X is the Roman numeral for ten, the ten-dollar bill was called a *sawbuck.*

Why do we say *brand-new?* This phrase has nothing to do with name brands, but goes back to the Middle Ages. Then a *brand* was a flame. When a metal product was taken out of the flames, it was *fire-new* or *brand-new.*

Why is it called a *dandelion?* The origin of *dandelion* is the French *dent de lion,* or "lion's tooth." The plant's jagged

1

leaves do in fact resemble the teeth of a lion, and several other European languages refer to the plant as "lion's tooth."

Why do we say *French leave*? *French leave* meant the same as "AWOL" (absent without leave) during World War I. Despite popular belief, the term has nothing to do with the lack of bravery of French soldiers. To the seventeenth-century French, it was perfectly proper to leave a party early without bidding formal farewell to the host and hostess; hence the term *French leave.*

Why is the weed called *tobacco*? Tobacco got its name from the pipe-smoking natives of Tobago, an island in the West Indies. The word *tobago* is the name of the Y-shaped tube used to inhale smoke from tobacco leaves.

Why do we say *jaywalker*? The word *jaywalker* originated from the word *jay*, which was a popular slang term meaning "rustic" during the early 1900s. A farmer, unaccustomed to the ways of the city, might cross a street without paying much attention to the signs, and be termed a *jaywalker.*

Why do we say *Indian giver*? The term *Indian giver* originated from one who gave a gift expecting to get a better one in return. It then came to be used to describe a gift that was later taken back by the giver.

Why is a group of subversives called a *fifth column*? This phrase, which became current in 1936, refers to people who secretly aid and abet the enemy. General Emilio Mola first used it during the Spanish Civil War. Leading four columns of rebels toward Madrid, he told newsmen he had a fifth column inside the city—an army of people who sympathized with him and would help his cause.

Why are they called *Harvard beets?* This dish of cooked beets warmed in a sauce of vinegar, sugar, and cornstarch got its name from Harvard University because its color resembled Harvard's school color, deep crimson red.

Where did the term *red herring* come from? The expression *red herring,* meaning any device used to confuse or divert attention, got its name from a hunting practice. A red herring dragged across a fox's trail destroys the fox's scent that has been laid and diverts the dogs' attention to a false trail.

Why is it called the *Latin Quarter?* This area in Paris, famous as a center of student life, got its name during the Middle Ages when tutors and students of the University of Paris conversed in Latin.

Why do we call the record of a meeting the *minutes?* Minutes of a meeting have nothing to do with time. The word stems from the Latin *minutus,* or "small." Records of meetings have always been written in miniature, or shorthand, and transcribed later.

Why is it called a *kangaroo court?* A *kangaroo court* is a mock court set up outside of established legal procedures. Institutions of this sort exist in most large prisons, where inmates fine and punish each other for various "infractions." The most plausible theory claims that the phrase originated in Australia, which at one time was a penal colony of the British Empire. The irregular proceedings of such unauthorized courts there were compared to the erratic leaps of the kangaroo.

Why do we say *roger?* The term *roger* comes from the earliest days of wireless communication when the letter *r* was used to indicate "OK—understood." Roger is voice code

3

for the letter *r* and is used as part of the "Able, Baker, Charlie" code known and used by all radiophone operators in the military. With the return of members of the armed forces to domestic life following World War II, *roger* came into common speech.

Why do we call police officers *cops?* Two theories account for this term. One points to the Old English verb "to cop," meaning "to catch." If this is the derivation, a police officer was originally a *copper,* or *cop* for short, in the sense that he or she cops or captures criminals. A more interest-

---

It Sounds Like a Lot of Bologna

The names of things often seem to have no rhyme or reason. For example, take food. In Denmark, Danish pastry is called Viennese bread. The British don't have English muffins. And if you order a frankfurter in Frankfurt, you'll get a small smoked sausage on a slice of bread. Of course, if you ask for a hamburger in Hamburg restaurants you'll be told, *"Ich bin ein Hamburger!"* Which means, "I am a Hamburger." And there's no chop suey in China; Spanish rice is not served in Spain, and turkey is not a common food in Turkey. But then, most Russians probably don't even know what Russian dressing is, nor are the people of France familiar with French toast. And Swiss cheese is not necessarily from Switzerland.

Back in the United States, a western sandwich is frequently called a Denver, which contains turkey, bacon, and tomatoes. Baked Alaska is not popular in our most northern state; and in New York, a New York steak is simply boneless sirloin. Boston lettuce is not necessarily from Boston.

A grapefruit has nothing to do with grapes, and pineapples have nothing to do with either pines or apples. Not all the names of food make a whole lot of sense, but thank heaven the color of an orange is orange!

---

ing theory refers to the time when Sir Robert Peel organized the first modern police force. He dressed the men
in blue uniforms with conspicuous copper buttons. These
buttons, some say, led to the nickname *coppers*, later shortened to *cops*.

Why is a heavy reader called a *bookworm*? There actually
are bookworms. Found in old, undusted libraries, they are
the larvae of insects that feed on the paste in book bind-
ings. Because they are always found around books—and
sometimes seem to "devour" them—avid readers are
called *bookworms*.

Why does a person go *scot-free*? The expression *scot-free*,
used to mean "without payment of a just penalty," and
comes from Elizabethan England, where a scot was a municipal tax paid to the bailiff. Thus, those scoundrels who
managed to successfully evade paying their taxes got off
scot-free.

Why do we use the term *lame duck*? A *lame duck* is an of-
ficeholder who has lost the election for the next term but
still has some time to serve before a successor is inaugurated. The term comes to us from Exchange Alley,
eighteenth-century London's equivalent of Wall Street.
There, people who couldn't pay their debts were referred
to as *lame ducks* because, it was said, they "waddled out of
the Alley."

Where did the term *swan song* originate? A *swan song* refers
to the last great work of a creative artist, be he or she a
poet, writer, painter, or musician. The expression comes
from the legend that every swan sings one glorious song
just before his death. Ironically, a swan doesn't sing.

Why is a football field called a *gridiron*? A *gridiron* is a flat framework of parallel metal bars that can be placed over a flame for broiling food. A football field, with its rectangular shape and parallel white lines, resembles this device. The famous Gridiron Club in Washington, D.C., is so named because at dinners the members satirize—that is, put over a flame, or "roast"—important figures.

Why do we call it a *drawing room*? Originally, a drawing room was not a place to sketch, but rather a place to which one could withdraw. *Withdrawing room* was later contracted to *drawing room.*

Why is the sale of illegal liquor called *bootlegging*? The sale of illegal liquor originated in the West, when it was unlawfully sold on reservations to the Indians. Often, flasks of liquor were carried in the violator's boots in order to conceal the merchandise from government officials. When Prohibition laws were passed in various parts of the country, the term *bootlegging* was applied to the illegal sale of liquor.

Why is it called a *funny bone*? If a nerve is pressed at a specific point in the elbow, a painful, tingling sensation results. Why, then, is it called the *funny bone*? One reasonable conjecture is that it is a play on the Latin word *humerus,* which is the medical name of the long bone in the upper arm.

Why are they called *sperm whales*? Early whalers found massive loads of mysterious waxy stuff in whales' snouts. Thinking it was the whales' reproductive extract, they named the substance *spermaceti,* meaning "seed of the whale." In fact, the substance has no reproductive function, assisting instead as part of the whale's sonar mechanism and possibly as a protective cushion against deep-sea pressure.

Why is the Chinese dish called *chop suey?* In Chinese, *chop suey* means miscellaneous bits of food, like hash. In New York, on August 29, 1896, the Chinese statesman Li Hung-Chang had his chef create *chop suey*, which at that time was unknown in China. He hoped to create a dish that would appeal to both American and Asian tastes.

Why do we say *Dixie?* *Dixie* may be derived simply from the Mason-Dixon line (the boundary still sometimes used to distinguish the South from the North). But a more ingenious explanation traces it to *dix,* the French word for "ten." *Dix* used to be displayed in large letters on a bilingual ten-dollar bill issued by a bank in New Orleans, and the bills gained the nickname *dixies.* Since having ten dollars in the South's most colorful city was a pleasant sensation, some Southerners saw *Dixie* as a positive name for the South. When Daniel Emmet's song "Dixie" became popular in 1859, the term rapidly spread throughout the country.

Where did the word *Jeep* come from? This term is believed to have developed from the abbreviation "GP" used by the army for "general purpose" vehicle. Its immediate acceptance can be credited to Eugene the Jeep, a comic strip character with supernatural powers, created by E. C. Segar, a popular cartoonist during the years preceding World War II.

Why do card players call the pot *kitty?* In many card games, players pool their winnings in a *kitty.* The term is believed to have originated from the word *kit,* which was used commonly as far back as 1400. *Kit* was used to refer to a vessel, blanket, bag, or other type of container; soldiers carried their money in a kit.

Why are they called *dog days?* It was once thought that dog days were the time of the year when dogs were more likely to become rabid. Actually, statistics show that most cases of rabies among dogs occur in early spring and late fall. This belief probably grew out of the phrase *dog days*, rather than the other way around. The ancient Greeks and Romans applied the name *dog days* to the period between July 3 and August 11, when the Dog Star, Sirius, rises at the same time as the sun. The ancients thought this conjunction was responsible for the heat and drought of midsummer.

Why is a can opener called a *church key*? Many people suppose the term *church key*, describing the kind of opener that punches a triangle in a can of beer, reflects a mock reverence for the brew. Actually, the present church key replaced an older kind of bottle opener of the same name. That device looked like the top end of one of the large, ornate keys used to open church doors. When cans became popular, today's church key gained in popularity, and the name was transferred to it.

Why do golfers say *take a mulligan*? The term *take a mulligan*, used when your golf partner gives you a free shot when yours goes bad, got its start in the saloons of yesteryear. According to one theory, there was always a bottle of mulligan on the bar of the old-time saloons. The basic ingredients were hot pepper seeds and water. A few drops of the solution in your beer would eat out your liver, stomach, bladder, and heart, which is exactly what happens when you accept a mulligan.

Why are a pair of aces with a pair of eights called a *dead man's hand* in poker? It is believed that when James Butler Hickok ("Wild Bill") was shot by Jack McCall during a poker game in Deadwood, South Dakota, on August 2, 1876, he held such a hand. Although it was an unfortunate event for law-enforcement officer Hickok, many poker players believe that a dead man's hand is very lucky and is seldom beaten.

Why do we call enthusiasts *fans*? A *fan*, meaning a devoted admirer of a sport, athletic team, famous person, etc., is a contraction of *fanatic*. The word seems to have originated in the 1880s when Chris Van der Ahe, owner of the St. Louis Browns, referred to Charles Haas as a baseball fanatic. Sportswriters found the word appealing and began to call all baseball followers fanatics. The headline writers shortened the word, for convenience, to *fans*. The term was so useful that it was applied to ardent enthusiasts in other sports and the entertainment field.

Where did the term *benchmark* come from? You might suppose that the first *bench mark* was a line on a carpenter's bench for purposes of measuring. In fact, it was originally a surveyor's term, referring to any permanent part of the landscape, such as a rock outcropping. A bench mark has a known position and known altitude, and can therefore be used as a reference point to determine other altitudes. The term *benchmark* is now used to mean something that serves as a standard for measuring achievement.

Why do we use the word *serendipity*? *Serendipity* comes from an old Persian fairy tale, "The Three Princes of Serendip," recounted in 1754 by the British author Horace Walpole. The three princes in the story were always discovering things they were not looking for. The word *serendipity* means finding things of value that were not sought for.

Why do we call the breakfast food *cereal*? This everyday word comes from Roman mythology. The goddess Ceres ruled over grain, the harvest, and all agriculture. When the great drought of 496 B.C. ended, the Romans believed Ceres had answered their prayers for rain. They built numerous temples to her and established annual festivals in her honor. The grain was known in Latin as *cerealis*, "of Ceres." The word *cereal* includes all edible grains, but is more commonly used to refer to what we eat for breakfast.

Why is it called *moonshine*? *Moonshine* is generally associated with homemade stills in the mountain districts of Kentucky, Tennessee, Virginia, and North Carolina. Many people think the whiskey from these stills was called moonshine because it had to be made at night to evade revenue officers. Actually, the term may not be American at all. In an English dictionary dated 1785, *moonshine* is defined as white brandy smuggled into England at night.

Why is a group of affiliated companies called a *conglomerate*? In geology, the term *conglomerate* means a rock composed of pebbles and gravel embedded in some kind of cementing material. A group of companies that constitute a single corporation is accordingly called a *conglomerate*.

Why is a stiff muscle called a *charley horse*? Anyone can get a *charley horse*, although it is more common among athletes who use their muscles strenuously. Overstrained muscles suddenly contract into a stiff knot, and any exercise is very painful. The term derives from an old American custom of calling any old horse, especially one with stiff legs, a charley horse.

Why do we say *chauffeur*? Any student of French knows that *chauffeur* means "to warm up." Why, then, do chauffeurs have that name? The first automobile drivers in France drove steam-propelled vehicles. Their job began with heating up the engine until enough steam was generated to propel the car. Thus, they were called chauffeurs, or "warmers."

Why are first- and second-year students called *freshmen* and *sophomores*? The word *freshman* goes back to 1550, when a first-year university student was fresh—untried and inexperienced. And he was a man; college in those days was definitely not for women. Because of this origin, many feminists prefer *first-year student* or even *freshperson*. *Sophomore* is equally interesting in its origin. The Greek *sophos* meant "wise," and *moros* meant "foolish." It is well known, or assumed at least, that, based on their newfound experience, sophomores are given to making confident pronouncements on weighty issues, while in fact they are quite immature and relatively unlearned.

Why are small coins called *pennies*? There has never been an official penny in the United States. The congressional act creating this coin refers to it as a cent, a name that comes from the Latin *centum*, or "hundred." But the English penny was widely used here until a law in 1787 banned all foreign currency from circulation. Thereafter the cent took on the name *penny*. Because it was the old English currency, the word *penny* appears in a number of folk sayings, such as "A penny for your thoughts" and "Penny wise and pound foolish." The word *penny* itself probably comes from the Latin *pannus*, or "cloth"; in barbarian Europe, pieces of cloth were used as a means of exchange.

Why is a naive person called a *sucker*? The comparison here is to any young animal that is not yet weaned. Someone who is easily deceived or gullible is said to be, like an infant, a *sucker*, although certainly one does not have a helpless newborn in mind when such name-calling is used. The term implies that the sucker is not only gullible, but stupid as well!

Why do we use the terms *starboard* and *port*? If you face forward on a ship, starboard is on your right. Anglo-Saxon

11

vessels were steered with an oar held on that side. *Steor* meant "rudder" in Old English, and *bord* meant the "side of the boat." So the rudder side was the *steorbord*. It may be that *port* was adopted for the left side because boats were anchored at harbor with the steering oar away from the dock and the left side against the wharf, or facing port.

Why is an informer called a *stool pigeon?* When a person squeals on somebody, he or she is often referred to as a *stool pigeon*. This expression originates from the old practice of tying pigeons to a stool, or perch, to lure other pigeons into the hunters' snares.

Why is gossip called *scuttlebutt?* The original *scuttlebutt* was a shipboard cask that contained the crew's drinking water. Just as modern workers gather around office drinking fountains, sailors gathered around the scuttlebutt to exchange gossip.

Why do we say *scapegoat?* Originally this word represented just what it seems to mean: an "escape goat." On the Day of Atonement, the ancient Jews would bring two goats to the altar. The high priest chose one to be sacrificed. Then he confessed the sins of the congregation over the head of the second. After that, the goat was taken to the edge of the village and allowed to escape into the wilderness, taking all the people's sins with it. That was the first *scapegoat*. Now the word describes a person who, like that ancient goat, is blamed for other people's mistakes.

Why is it called a *round robin?* A round robin is a tournament in which each contestant plays every other contestant. Its name has nothing to do with the bird, but comes from *ruban*, French for "ribbon." The first round robin was devised in eighteenth-century France, where the king, if angered by a petition, was likely to have the first signer beheaded. Naturally, nobody wanted to be first. Finally

someone came up with the idea of having all the petitioners sign a ribbon and then joining the ribbon in a circle.
Thus, nobody's name was first on the list! A similar device
originated in the British navy, where the ship's captain
could order hanged the first signer of a petition of griev-
ance, who was assumed to be the leader. The signatures of
the petitioners were thus arranged in a circle, like the
spokes of a ship's wheel.

Why is an unknown person called *John Doe?* In legal actions
we refer to an unknown person as *John Doe* or *Jane Doe.*
This began in England as early as the fourteenth century.
The name sounds like a common one, as it was undoubt-
edly meant to, but is in fact very uncommon, which helps
avoid confusion.

Why are marines referred to as *leathernecks?* At least two
explanations are given for this term. The first, and least
flattering, is a navy tradition. Sailors believed that early marines did not strip to the waist to wash, as sailors did, but
only rolled up their sleeves and washed their hands and
faces. Thus, *leatherneck* described a dirty, long-unwashed
neck. A more likely explanation is that the name was suggested by marine uniforms of the nineteenth century. The
regulation coat had a high, close-fitting collar lined with
leather to keep it stiff. Because these collars were very un-
comfortable when wet with perspiration, they were abandoned in the last quarter of the century. The term
leatherneck, however, persists.

Why do we refer to unwanted items as *white elephants?* A
white elephant is an Indian elephant of a pale gray or
yellowish color. Such animals have been considered sacred
in many countries, including Siam. A popular explanation
of the term *white elephant,* meaning something that is expensive to maintain, is that the King of Siam would give

such an animal to a nobleman he wished to bring down. The nobleman would, of course, have to maintain the animal in style, and would go broke in the process. There is, however, no evidence to support this theory of the word's origin. In fact, only the king was considered worthy of owning a white elephant, so all such animals were brought to him alone. The animals were kept in special stables, their only value being their significance as a symbol of royal dignity. That these useless animals should be so expensively maintained led to the term *white elephant.*

Why is the vegetable called an *Irish potato*? The Irish potato was named after the Irish because they depended so greatly on the potato for food. When disease destroyed the potato crop in the 1840s, famine resulted and thousands of Irish people left their homeland for the New World. Actually, the potato should have been named a Venezuelan or Argentinean potato because it was first cultivated in South America, where the Indians had grown it for many centuries before it was introduced in Europe around 1570.

Why do Mexicans refer to an American as a *gringo*? *Gringo* is a contemptuous Mexican word for foreigners, especially Americans and the English. Most experts agree that it comes from the Spanish *griego,* meaning "Greek." This was used in the sense of gibberish, as Americans say, "It's all Greek to me." Another theory, however, traces the word to Major Samuel Ringgold, who fought in the Mexican War under Zachary Taylor. His bravery was well known, and he and his flying artillery corps were widely feared by Mexican marauders. When Ringgold is pronounced with a Spanish accent, it sounds much like *gringo.*

Why is it called *Gothic* architecture? The Goths actually had nothing to do with this form of architecture. The architecture of the Middle Ages was not called Gothic until the Renaissance, when painters and writers began to use the term as a way of expressing contempt for such architecture, which they thought barbaric.

Why is the color called *khaki*? The word derives from the Persian *khak*, meaning "earth" or "dust." It entered the language by way of the British occupation of India. The first British troops in that country wore regulation red or white uniforms—very conspicuous in the dry season, when dust turned everything brown. Since the bright colors made the soldiers perfect targets for snipers, the uniforms were soon made of khaki, or earth-colored, cloth, first in India, later worldwide.

Why is a golf course referred to as *links*? *The Art of Golfe,* written in 1892 by Sir W. J. Simpson, stated: "The grounds on which golf is played are called links, being the barren sandy soil from which the sea has retired in recent geological times. In their natural state, links are covered with long, rank, bent grass and gorse. These links are too barren for cultivation, but sheep, rabbits, geese and professionals pick up a precarious livelihood on them." Of course, today some of the best links are found in deserts and mountainous areas throughout the world.

Why is underwear called *BVDs*? There have been a lot of theories about what these letters stand for. Some said "Baby's Ventilated Diapers" and some said "Boy's Ventilated Drawers." But the simple truth is that these initials stand for the names of the men who founded the company in 1876: Bradley, Voorhies, and Day.

Why is a very short haircut called a *crew cut*? The *crew cut* is so named because oarsmen commonly wore this cool and trouble-free hairstyle. The very short haircut has also

15

had other names. Since it was the favored style of Paul von Hindenburg, president of Germany from 1925 to 1934, it was known as a "Hindenburg haircut." Later, it was called a "military cut." But before that time, anyone who wanted such a style went to a livery stable. There, using a horse clipper, the stableman would give a "pig shave cut," both words reflecting its appearance.

Why are golf bag carriers called *caddies?* Mary, who became Queen of Scots in 1542, was an avid golfer. As a young girl she was sent to France to be educated. She referred to the ball chasers as "cadets"—the young pupils who carried her golf clubs. In French, *cadets* is pronounced "cad-day," and the term *caddie* was soon adopted. It is not known what these golf ballboys were called before Mary's visit to France.

Why were Asian laborers called *coolies?* *Kuli* was the name of an Indian caste whose members hired out as unskilled labor, carrying burdens, bricks, and earth. Europeans in India took to calling all unskilled laborers "kulis," an Indian word. Some authorities think the term *coolie* derives from this usage. Others think it is a combination of two Chinese words: *koo* ("painful") and *lee* ("strength"). In any case, in the early nineteenth century the term came to be applied specifically to unskilled workers from Asia.

Where did the word *free-lancer* **come from?** It's been said that a free-lancer is any newspaper reporter who's out of work! The free lances of the Middle Ages, however, really carried lances. They were professional soldiers—sometimes led by a knight—who were hired out as mercenaries to feudal lords. They were first described as free-lancers around 1820. Since that time the term has broadened to include any person who sells his or her services without a long-term commitment.

Why are fried potatoes called *French fries*? It seems odd to many people that the only place in France where you can get "French fries" is at an American hamburger stand. Actually, however, the origin of this popular food is probably British. In England, fried potatoes are served with fish and are called "chips." The American name, *French fries*, reflects the method of preparation. Any meat or vegetable that is cut into narrow strips before cooking is said to be "Frenched." So Frenched and fried potatoes have become simply French fries.

Why was the Model T called the *Tin Lizzie*? Introduced in 1908, the Model T (which was simply the design that followed the Model S) was produced until 1927. More than 15 million were built. The car was so popular that the Ford Motor Company periodically had to refuse orders in order to catch up on its backlog.

The Model T was not made of tin but rather of sheet metal; it was initially called the "tin car" only because it was built for the masses, as other Fords had been. Why "Lizzie"? In those days many families employed a domestic servant, who might typically be named Lizzie. Like her, the Model T helped do everything six days a week, then got prettied up on Sunday and took off. In time, the "tin car" came to be compared to the family domestic—thus, the *Tin Lizzy*.

Why is a long shot called a *dark horse*? Benjamin Disraeli, the distinguished nineteenth-century English prime minister, was also a well-known writer. Among his works was a three-volume novel, *The Young Duke: A Moral Tale Though Gay*. In volume 2, the book's main character attends a horse race. He is amazed to see "a dark horse" he hadn't noticed before sweep past the judges' box to win first place. During the time this novel was popular, the dark horse the

17

duke observed came to stand for any winner whose victory no one predicts. And it still has the same meaning.

Why are they called *midshipmen*? Young men in the British navy who were training to become officers were always quartered on the lower deck—amidships. Thus, cadets and low-ranking officers came to be called "midshipmen," the term still used at Annapolis.

Why is a small town called a *jerkwater town*? In the early days of railroads, trains stopped at wayside streams for water. The practice was called "jerking water" because the water was carried in leather buckets, or "jerked," to the train. The original jerkwater town had nothing to recommend it except that trains could refill their water supply there. So *jerkwater* has come to be applied to any small or insignificant place.

Why do we call it a *jackrabbit*? *Jackrabbit* comes from "jackass rabbit." This does not refer to the way the animal acts, but to its long ears, which are similar to those of the jackass. In the Old West it was sometimes called the mule rabbit and sometimes—in a tribute to size—the Texas hare. But *jackass rabbit* caught on, and was eventually shortened to *jackrabbit*.

Where did *baker's dozen* come from? Bread baking and selling were tightly regulated in England during the Middle Ages. It may be that this phrase grew out of some bakers' custom of giving an extra loaf with each dozen so that they would not be fined for underweight. An older name for 13 was "Devil's dozen," a reference to the belief that witches gather in covens of 13 to receive orders from the Devil.

How did the days of the week get their names? For much of history there was no week—calendars were simply arranged

Peculiar Plurals of Creatures

Groups of creatures often have highly unusual names, as in:

an army of frogs	a murder of crows
a business of ferrets	an exaltation of larks
a pride of lions	a nide of pheasants
a skulk of foxes	a convocation of eagles
a gang of elks	a gaggle of geese (on the ground)
a troop of monkeys	a skein of geese (in flight)
a troop of kangaroos	a bed of oysters
a husk of hares	a pod of whales, as well as a gam
a clutter of cats	of whales
a sleuth of bears	a pod of seals, as well as a gam
a trip of goats	of seals
a clutch of chickens	

around lunar months. Our week derives from the fact that the Babylonians held market days every seventh day. The Jews copied this custom and added the Sabbath, also observed every seventh day. The Jews first named the week using numbers, with Saturday, the Sabbath, as day seven. The Romans adopted the seven-day week and named it after the Egyptian system—one day for the sun, one for the moon, and one for each of the five known planets. The names we use were derived from the Anglo-Saxons, who patterned their names on those of the Romans. Thus the day of the sun became *Sunnandaeg* (Sunday). The day of the moon was *Monandaeg* (Monday). Tuesday was *Tiwesdaeg*, after Tiw, their god of war. The next day had been named after Mercury, but the Anglo-Saxons named it for the god *Woden* (Wednesday). Jupiter, the thunderer, became *Thor*, the thunder god (Thursday). The next day honored *Frigg*

19

or *Freya,* wife of Odin (Friday). The day of Saturn was *Saeternsdaeg* (Saturday). Incidentally, at one time a day was counted as the space between sunrise and sunset. It was the Romans who conceived of a day as running from midnight to midnight, the method now used.

PROPER NAMES
THAT BECAME WORDS

■

Many words in our language are derived from the names of people. These words are so commonly used today that we make no connection with the person from whom the word originated. How many times, for example, have you associated the game of *craps* with a specific individual? Or, for that matter, put on a cardigan sweater knowing it was named after a British lord. There are dozens of "people" words included in this chapter, so read on and discover "who" became "what"!

Atlas. *Atlas* was one of the Titans who made war on Zeus and were defeated by him. As a punishment, Zeus gave Atlas the job of holding up the heavens forever. In the sixteenth century, noted geographer Gerardus Mercator teamed up with John Hondt and published *Atlas: Or a Geographic Description of the World,* and mapmakers began putting together collections of maps with the figure of Atlas on them.

Big Ben. *Big Ben* is often thought to be a large clock in London. In fact, it isn't. Big Ben is the bell that rings out the hour in Parliament tower. This bell, which weighs 13 tons, was named after Sir Benjamin Hall, chief commissioner of public works at the time it was installed, because of his size.

Bobby. When British statesman Sir Robert Peel became home secretary, he created the London police force. Citizens believed the force was created to suppress legitimate discontent and called it "Peel's bloody gang." Later the police were called "Peelers" and "bobbies" (Bobby is a nickname of Robert), and as time passed, the diminutives lost their derogatory impact. Today the people of Great Britain affectionately call their police *bobbies.*

Booze. Some people believe the word *booze* goes back to the Philadelphia distiller E. S. Booz, whose name appears on old whiskey bottles. But the word was already in use in the fourteenth century, when "to booze" meant "to drink heavily." Incidentally, while Americans use *booze* to mean hard liquor, the English use it to mean beer or ale.

Boycott. This word comes from the name of Captain Charles Boycott. In 1880, when he attempted to collect high rents from the earl of Earne's poor tenants, the Irish farmers ignored, or *boycotted,* the captain.

Bunsen burner. The *Bunsen burner,* most often found in science laboratories, was invented by German chemist Robert Wilhelm Bunsen, a nineteenth-century professor at Heidelberg.

Caesarean section. Many people think this operation was so named because Julius Caesar was delivered by this method. In fact, he was not. The Romans did not perform this operation on living women, though Roman law did permit such an operation after the mother's death so the child might be delivered live, which occasionally happened, or so that the mother or child could be buried separately, as religion dictated. This law was part of a group of laws codified in 715 B.C., which, under the reign of the emperors, came to be known as the Caesarean Laws. The specific law that pertained to the childbirth operation was called the *Caesarean Section*. The word *section* comes from the Latin *sectus*, "to cut."

Caesar salad. Caesar Cardini, who operated a string of restaurants in Tijuana in the 1920s and 1930s, created this delightful salad. His ingredients were romaine lettuce, garlic, olive oil, Worcestershire sauce, Parmesan cheese, croutons, and a coddled egg. He did not favor the anchovies that were later added by other chefs.

Cardigan. During the Crimean War, Britain's Lord Cardigan was brigadier general in command of the Light Brigade. He distinguished himself greatly by his courage in the doomed battle of Balaklava, in what became known as the Charge of the Light Brigade. When he returned home he was cheered for his heroism and invited to stay at Windsor Castle. The woolen jacket he had worn during the campaign was named a *cardigan* and became widely popular.

Casanova. Born into a theatrical family in Venice, Giovanni Giacomo Casanova (1725–1798) really did live and was widely known for his amorous escapades. As a consequence, a man who has a reputation as a great lover is called a *Casanova.*

Chauvinism. Nicolas Chauvin was a soldier in Napoleon's army. After being wounded 17 times he was retired on a meager pension. Nevertheless, Chauvin was fanatically devoted to Napoleon and praised him constantly. *Chauvinist* came to mean anyone who is blindly loyal to a group, especially to his country.

Chicken à la king. While there are dozens of stories that explain this name, the two most persuasive ones suggest that the dish was originally "Chicken à la Keene." The London hotel Claridge's claims that its chef invented it in 1881 to honor sportsman J. R. Keene after his horse won the Grand Prix. But the New York restaurant Delmonico's has also been cited as the originator; there the dish was supposed to have been suggested by Keene's son, Foxhall. As numerous restaurants adopted the dish, many must have wanted to suggest that it was fit for royalty—hence, *Chicken à la king.*

Craps. Two theories explain how the game of *craps* got its name. One is that a Creole gambler, nicknamed Johnny Crapaud, introduced the game to New Orleans. There it became known as "Crapaud's game," later shortened to "craps." A second theory refers to an old dice game called "hazard." "Crabs," or "craps," in this game was the lowest possible throw. *Crap out* is still used the same way in the modern game, so this explanation seems more likely.

Derringer. The *derringer* is perhaps best known as the gun John Wilkes Booth used to shoot President Lincoln. The original derringer was a little box-lock pistol made by Henry Deringer, a gunsmith, in the late 1840s. So great was the demand for the gun that a California agent hired former apprentices of Deringer to make imitations of it. On the foreign imitations that soon appeared, *Derringer* was spelled with two *r*'s. The latter spelling is now standard, referring to any short-barreled pistol.

Doily. During the early eighteenth century, a Londoner named Doily amassed a fortune from selling linens and crocheted goods. His fast rise to riches became so famous that the *doily* was named after him.

Doubting Thomas. The term *doubting Thomas* came from St. Thomas, one of the 12 apostles who, according the Scripture, doubted Christ's crucifixion and demanded to see the marks on Christ's body (John 20:24–29). After Christ had appeared before Thomas and convinced him, he said: "Thomas, because thou hast seen me, thou hast believed; blessed are they that have not seen, and yet have believed."

Douglas fir. These tall evergreens, also known as Douglas spruce, were named after David Douglas, an explorer and botanist from Scotland who discovered the tree on an expedition in the United States in 1825.

Dukes. The slang term *dukes,* meaning fists, has an odd origin. The duke of Wellington boasted such a large nose that *duke* became a synonym for *nose.* Then, so the theory goes, a man's fist became a "duke buster." "Put up your dukes" has long been a familiar expression meaning "Get ready to fight!"

Eggs Benedict. Samuel Benedict, a prominent New Yorker, is credited with creating this famous high-calorie breakfast dish. One morning at the old Waldorf-Astoria Hotel, he ordered poached eggs, bacon, and toast with hollandaise sauce. Oscar, the maitre d', suggested substituting a muffin and a slice of ham for the toast and bacon. Benedict was pleased with the results, as was Oscar, who christened it *eggs Benedict* and added it to the menu.

Fahrenheit. This temperature scale was named after a thermometer-maker of the late eighteenth century, Daniel Gabriel Fahrenheit. Ever since, freezing has been measured at 32 degrees *Fahrenheit* and the boiling point is measured at 212 degrees Fahrenheit.

Flowers Named After People

Begonia. The begonia was named after the French governor of Santo Domingo, Michel Bégon (1638–1710).

Camellia. The camellia was named after George Josef Kamel (1661–1706), a Moravian Jesuit missionary.

Dahlia. The dahlia was named after Anders Dahl, an eighteenth-century Swedish botanist.

Fittonia. Botanists Elizabeth and Sarah Fitton named this flower.

Fuchsia. The fuchsia was named by Carolus Linnaeus after a German botanist, Leonhard Fuchs (1501–1566).

Lobelia. Matthias de Lobel (1538–1616), a Flemish botanist, named this flower.

Magnolia. This beautiful flower was named after Pierre Magnol, a seventeenth-century professor of botany at Montpellier University in France. He was one of the first to classify plants by families.

Poinsettia. The poinsettia was discovered by J. R. Poinsett (1799–1851), the U.S. minister to Mexico, home of this flowering plant.

Wisteria. This flower was named after Casper Wistar (1761–1818), an American anatomist.

Zinnia. The zinnia was named after Johann Gottfried Zinn (1729–1759), a German botanist.

Ferris wheel. This amusement park ride got its name from George W. G. Ferris, who designed the first one for the Columbian Exposition in Chicago in 1893. Ever since, at amusement parks and carnivals all over the world, the *Ferris wheel* has been one of the most popular rides for people of all ages.

Garrison finish. The *Garrison finish* was named after jockey Edward H. Garrison who was famous for his practice of holding his horse far back in the pack, and moving up with a rush only when entering the home stretch.

Gaudy. The word *gaudy* traces back to the Middle English word *gaude,* referring to a large bead in a rosary or trinket. Linguists suspect that the original root is *gaudium,* the Latin word for joy. Today, gaudy refers to anything showy and ostentatious. A gaudy is also a feast, particularly an annual dinner held at a British university, a usage that also harks back to the Latin for joy.

Gibson. A *Gibson* is a version of a martini, in which an onion is substituted for an olive. Charley Connerly, the head bartender at New York's famous Players Club, was making a martini for Dana Gibson and was temporarily out of olives so he substituted an onion and the Gibson was born.

Graham crackers. In the 1830s a Presbyterian minister named Sylvester Graham was an ardent advocate of temperance. He believed that not only must man abstain from drink, but that it was necessary to undo the effects of intemperance with a whole-grain vegetarian diet. Graham claimed that meat led to sexual excess, and mustard and ketchup brought on insanity. He also urged the substitution of whole-wheat bread for white. Graham food stores, much like today's health food stores, sprang up everywhere, and were violently opposed by butchers and bakers. Like all fads, this one soon came to an end. But modern science has proved Graham right in some respects. Americans do eat far too much meat, and the refining of flour does rob it of nutrients. Graham's followers called their whole-wheat flour "graham flour"; and crackers made from it were *graham crackers*, as they are today.

Great Scott. The expression *Great Scott* actually came from General Winfield Scott, hero of the Mexican War and one of America's most admired generals. This expression of surprise probably came as a tribute to his exploits. So while there have been many great military leaders, there has been only one Great Scott.

Guillotine. It is commonly supposed that the *guillotine* was named after its inventor, but that is not the case. It wasn't even called a guillotine when it was first used in France. The instrument was an adaptation of an Italian device and was named the "Louison" after its adaptor, a Dr. Louis. Dr. Joseph Guillotin's contribution was to help push through the French National Assembly in 1792 a resolution adopting the guillotine as the official means of execution. He meant well, as it was quicker and more humane than the existing methods. First used to execute criminals, the machine became a political weapon during the Reign of Terror, when 8,000 French men and women died under its blade. Dr. Guillotin's family resented so strongly having their name attached to this instrument of terror that they officially changed the family name when he died.

Guy. *Guy* as a slang term for a man was not always as neutral as it is now. The word goes back to the famous Gunpowder Plot against the English Parliament in 1605. The conspirators, in retaliation against the oppression of Roman Catholics in Britain, placed 36 barrels of gunpowder in the basements of the Parliament buildings, planning to set them off on November 5, the day the king opened Parliament. But when Guy Fawkes went into the cellar to light the fuses, he was captured. The plot had become too widely known, and the conspiracy was revealed. November 5 became an English holiday, Guy Fawkes Day, celebrating the preservation of the government. Effigies of Fawkes were paraded through the streets and burned in huge bonfires. Celebrants customarily dressed in costumes similar to American Halloween costumes. A "guy" first meant any effigy, such as that of Guy Fawkes. Later it came to mean any odd-looking person. Over time, the term was used for "good guys" as well as "bad guys," until it became American slang for any man or group of people "you guys."

Hooligan. The word *hooligan* very likely comes from a rowdy boisterous Irish man from the late 1800s named Patrick Hooligan. We now use the word for a violent hoodlum or for rowdy behavior.

Hoyle (as in "according to . . ."). Edmond Hoyle (1672–1769) was an English writer on card games. It is believed that he earned his livelihood by playing card games, particularly whist, in taverns. In 1742 he published *A Short Treatise on the Game of Whist* and later wrote a general book on games. Hoyle was considered the foremost authority on whist, and later, games in general. Thus, playing a game *according to Hoyle* means that one is playing according to its recognized rules.

In like Flynn. The expression was named after Ed Flynn, who headed the Democratic Party machine in the 1940s. If you were in with Flynn, you had a good chance of being elected. He could also get you a soft job, put some pressure on somebody to get your real estate taxes lowered, and so on. All in all, he was a good man to have in your corner.

■

Hurricane Who?

Hurricanes are assigned names when they reach tropical storm strength, which is 39 miles per hour. Before hurricanes were given names, they were identified according to their latitude and longitude. This method was confusing and for a while they were identified by letters of the alphabet. Each letter had a name that corresponded with radio code words associated with each letter of the alphabet. To reduce confusion, in 1953, the National Weather Service began using female names to identify hurricanes. The list to be used each year was arranged in alphabetical order so that the name of the season's first hurricane began with the letter *A*, the second with *B*, and so on. The letters *Q, U, Y,* and *Z* are not used due to the scarcity of names beginning with these letters. The names are selected from library sources and then reviewed at an annual meeting of the World Meteorological Organization. The National Hurricane Center, which is located near Miami, Florida, makes the final decision on which names are used. Names are selected in advance for a six-year period. If a storm does great damage, its name is retired from the six-year list cycle.

Beginning in the late 1970s, hurricanes in the eastern Pacific as well as those in the North Atlantic were alternately assigned female and male names. The following are lists of the names of 1991–1994 Atlantic hurricanes:

1991	1992	1993	1994
Ana	Andrew	Arlene	Alberto
Bob	Bonnie	Bret	Beryl
Claudette	Charley	Cindy	Chris
Danny	Danielle	Dennis	Debby
Erika	Earl	Emily	Ernesto
Fabian	Frances	Floyd	Florence
Grace	George	Gert	Gordon
Henri	Hermione	Harvey	Helene
Isabel	Ivan	Irene	Isaac

1991	1992	1993	1994
Juan	Jeanne	Jose	Joan
Kate	Karl	Katrina	Keith
Larry	Lisa	Lenny	Leslie
Mindy	Mitch	Maria	Michael
Nicholas	Nicole	Nate	Nadine
Odette	Otto	Ophelia	Oscar
Peter	Paula	Philippe	Patty
Rose	Richard	Rita	Rafael
Sam	Shary	Stan	Sandy
Teresa	Thomas	Tammy	Tony
Victor	Virginia	Vince	Valerie
Wanda	Walter	Wilma	William

John Hancock. The biggest, boldest, and most defiant signature on the Declaration of Independence was scribbled by *John Hancock* of Massachusetts. Towering over the autographs of the other founding fathers, his name has become synonymous with *signature.*

Knickers. It's a long way from the early *knickers* to the knee-length breeches that bear that name today. The first knickers (when New York was still New Amsterdam) were clay bricks. The man who baked them was, of course, the "knicker baker." Like many other occupational names (such as Taylor and Mason), Knickerbaker became a family name, sometimes changed to Knickerbocker. Since the name was so common among the Dutch settlers, Washington Irving used it as the name of the invented author of his book *A History of New York,* Diedrich Knickerbocker. Illustrations in the book showed the old Dutchman wearing loose knee pants. Such breeches came to be called "knickerbockers," which was later shortened to "knickers."

31

Leotards. Leotards owe their popularity to a nineteenth-century French trapeze artist who wore the tight-fitting elastic garments for the torso and advocated them for men as "a more natural garb which does not hide your best features." His name? Jules Leotard. Today, women wear *leotards* more frequently than men—indicating, perhaps, that they, more than men, like to wear a more natural garb which does not hide their best features.

Macadam roads. *Macadam roads* were named after John L. MacAdam, a Scottish engineer who invented this method of paving roads during the late eighteenth century. A macadam road has a smooth surface made from small, broken stones that are rolled until solid.

Machiavellian. The word *machiavellian* was derived from Italian statesman and writer Niccolo Machiavelli (1469–1527), who advised rulers to use craftiness and deceit to maintain their authority. He outlined his strategies in the classic work, *The Prince.*

Mackintosh raincoats. Charles Mackintosh was the first man to make a truly waterproof fabric, and from him, we have *mackintosh raincoats.*

Mae West jackets. These inflatable life jackets that were responsible for saving thousands of airmen and sailors from drowning during World War II became known as *Mae West jackets* or just plain *Mae Wests.* Why? Because, like the buxom blonde bombshell, they bulged in the right places.

Manhattan. The *manhattan,* a potent cocktail made of whiskey and vermouth, was invented in the 1870s. It is named after its birthplace, a men's social club in New York City called the Manhattan Club.

Martini. The famous drink, the *martini,* got its name from the maker of vermouth, one of the cocktail's two ingredients. The name of the firm was Martini & Rossi.

Mason jar. John L. Mason invented *mason jars* in the late nineteenth century to preserve fruits and vegetables from the garden to eat during winter months.

Mesmerism. Oddly enough, Franz Anton Mesmer (1734–1815), who first used hypnotism, never realized what he was doing. This highly educated man first experimented with magnets, and found he could cure diseases ranging from stomachache to paralysis. But in further experiments he discovered that the cures occurred whether or not he held a magnet. His new skill, "animal magnetism," became the rage of Paris. In seancelike settings, patients would sit together listening to soft music. After an hour or so Mesmer would talk to each patient and stroke him or her with a little wand. The object was to produce a "crisis"— trembling, convulsions, fainting, even dancing—and it worked. At the height of his popularity, Mesmer was discredited by a commission appointed by France's Louis XVI, whose members included Benjamin Franklin. It was left to one of Mesmer's pupils to identify what his teacher had really done and call it *mesmerism.*

Molotov cocktail. The *Molotov cocktail* was used as an antitank weapon by the Soviets during World War II. It was simply a bottle filled with a flammable fluid such as gasoline and covered with a saturated rag. The rag was then lighted and the bottle was thrown at a tank or other target, spreading flames upon impact. This weapon was named for V. M. Molotov, Soviet minister of foreign affairs during the war.

Monkey wrench. Tradition has it that wrenches with adjustable moving jaws were invented by Charles Moncke, a London blacksmith. Since *Moncke* is pronounced almost like *monkey*, the name of the tool changed easily from "Moncke wrench" to *monkey wrench*.

Mud (as in "your name is . . ."). The American epithet *Your name is mud* was derived from Samuel Mudd, a doctor, who was found guilty of conspiracy in the assassination of President Abraham Lincoln. John Wilkes Booth showed up for treatment at Dr. Mudd's farmhouse near Bryantown, Maryland, on the morning after Lincoln's assassination.

Nicotine. *Nicotine* was named after a Frenchman named Jean Nicot, who introduced the tobacco plant to France in the late sixteenth century.

Oscar. For several years the trophies handed out annually by the Academy of Motion Picture Arts and Sciences were nameless. Margaret Herrick, librarian for the academy, supplied the name in 1931. When first shown the trophy she said, "It reminds me of my uncle Oscar." The name stuck.

Pap test. The *Pap test* got its name from a Greek-American anatomist and pathologist, George Papanicolaou. His smear test has saved thousands of women's lives since the 1940s by diagnosing cervical cancer in its curable stages.

Pasteurization. This process was invented by Louis Pasteur, a French chemist in the nineteenth century. Before pasteurization, people could become deathly ill from drinking milk.

Peeping Tom. Any person who spies on others—for example, someone who peeks at night into a house—is called a *Peeping Tom*. The phrase goes back to the story of Lady Godiva. Her husband, the lord of Coventry, levied high tolls on his subjects. A kindhearted woman, she appealed to him so often to abolish these taxes that he agreed to do so if she would ride naked through the village. Deciding to call his bluff, she sent out a proclamation asking the townspeople to stay indoors behind closed shutters while she rode. Everyone did, except Tom the tailor, who peeped through a hole in the shutter. According to the legend, he was immediately stricken blind. Lady Godiva's husband kept his promise and abolished the tolls, but *Peeping Tom* came into the language to memorialize the foolish tailor.

Phillips screw. The *Phillips screw* head is named after its inventor, Henry F. Phillips, who patented it in 1936. The Phillips screwdriver was named the same way.

Pompadour. The hairstyle was so named because a beautiful mistress of Louis XV, Madame de Pompadour, wore her golden hair swept straight up from the forehead. She is believed to have had such beauty and intellectual charm that the king gave her a room in the palace itself. Although she died in her early forties, the marquise de Pompadour's unusual hairstyle became a household word that has long outlived her otherwise illustrious reputation.

Pullman car. The *Pullman car* got its name from George M. Pullman, who built the first successful train sleeping car, the Pullman Palace Car. Pullman cars were a luxury for the very rich and powerful during the years when Americans traveled cross-country by railway. However, the era of long-distance railroad passenger cars has since given way to the much quicker way to go—by jet plane.

Pumpernickel bread. The German rye bread called *pumpernickel* was so named by Napoleon Bonaparte. He didn't particularly care for the bread, insisting that it was fit only for his horse, Nicole. As he expressed himself in French, *pain pour Nicole.*

Ritzy. The name comes from Cesar Ritz (1850–1918), who, in his day, was the most famous hotelier in the world. Ritz was Swiss born but began his hotel career in Paris. He later managed London's Savoy Hotel and then formed his own company, building the famous Ritz Hotel on Paris's Place Vendome in 1898.

Salisbury steak. In 1886, British physician James Salisbury stipulated that well-done ground beef eaten three times a day with a glass of hot water before and after each meal would be a cure-all for pulmonary tuberculosis, hardening of the arteries, gout, colitis, asthma, bronchitis, rheumatism, and pernicious anemia. Sorry James, but this so-called *Salisbury steak* is nothing more than a hamburger without a bun.

Saxophone. Antoine J. Sax was a very successful maker of musical instruments. Before he was 30 years old he invented a series of brass instruments that gave a new tone quality. In 1846 his inventions were registered and given the name *Saxophones*.

Scrooge. The word *scrooge* used for a stingy person comes from Ebenezer Scrooge, the greedy leading character in Dickens's *A Christmas Carol*.

Sequoia. These giant redwood trees found in California and southern Oregon were named after Sequoyah, an Indian leader in the early 1800s. His name in the Cherokee language was *Sikwo ya*.

Shrapnel. The lethal metal fragments of a modern hand grenade, called *shrapnel*, are named after a British ordnance officer, Henry Shrapnel (1762–1842). He was the inventor of the shrapnel shot that was first used by George III's troops when they invaded Dutch Surinam.

Sideburns. The original name was "burnsides," after Ambrose E. Burnside, a Civil War general who wore long side whiskers with a shaved chin. Because this style included whiskers on the sides of the face, the syllables were soon transposed into *sideburns*.

Sousaphone. The *Sousaphone* (a type of tuba) got its name when John Philip Sousa (1854–1923), who was known as the "March King," started using the huge-belled, oom-pah-pah instrument in his popular marching bands. Sousa is known for his great marching music that includes "Stars and Stripes Forever."

Spoonerism. A *spoonerism* is an error of speech, or a transposition of sounds from one word to another. Rev. William Archibald Spooner (1844–1930), who taught at Oxford University, is credited with having invented the spoonerism. He was said to have described Queen Victoria as "our queer old dean." And once he is reported to have shouted at students: "You have tasted the whole worm. You have hissed by mystery lectures. You were fighting a liar in the quad. You will leave by the town drain."

Stetson. The hat got its name from its creator, John Batterson Stetson (1830–1906), who was the son of a New Jersey milliner and later moved to the Colorado gold fields. Stetson returned east in 1865 and opened a hat factory in Philadelphia. His company specialized in designing hats that appealed to the tastes he acquired during his years out west. At the time of his death, *Stetson* hats were selling at a rate of 2 million a year.

Teddy bear. Toy bears became popular in Germany around the turn of the century. In the fall of 1902 they were imported into the United States. At about that time President Teddy Roosevelt went on a hunting trip in Mississippi. It was reported that he refused to shoot a small bear that was brought into his camp for that purpose. Cartoonist Clifford Berryman was inspired by this and drew a cartoon of the incident, labeling it "Drawing the Line in Mississippi." The public, highly amused by the whole thing, began to associate the popular toy bears with Teddy's hunting adventures, and the term *Teddy bear* became nationally known.

Uncle Sam. There is no better personification of the United States government than *Uncle Sam*. Supposedly the figure originated during the war of 1812. One Samuel Wilson, a merchant in the slaughtering business in Troy, New York, shipped large quantities of meat and other commodities to American forces stationed in various places in the North. Soldiers from Troy recognized the origin of the shipments by the packaging and jokingly spoke of the meat as "Uncle Sam's beef." This expression was quickly adopted by their fellow soldiers and applied to all property of the United States government. Now it is a synonym for the U.S. government itself.

Windsor knot. This massive and unwieldy knot for men's ties was named after the British duke of Windsor, Edward VIII—the same Briton who abdicated his throne in 1936 when he made Wallis Simpson his duchess. The well-dressed Windsor tied a larger-than-normal knot and others emulated him.

THE MOST COMMON NAMES IN AMERICA

■

One thing is for sure, the popularity of names changes like fashion. What was *in* way back when is *out* today. For instance, names like Max, Horace, Mildred, and Beatrice conjure up images of elderly people while names like Brad, Jeff, Nicole, and Tiffany sound like young people. Here are the ten most popular male and female names in the United States at various times:

MALE

1876	1900s	1976	1987
William	John	Michael	Michael
John	William	David	Christopher
Charles	Charles	John	Jonathan
Harry	Robert	Christopher	Daniel
James	Joseph	Joseph	David
George	James	Anthony	Anthony
Frank	George	Robert	Joseph
Robert	Samuel, Thomas	Jason	Matthew
Joseph	Arthur	James	John
Thomas	Harry	Daniel	Andrew

Of the above, only John and Joseph made the list every time.

FEMALE

1896	1900s	1976	1987
Mary	Mary	Jennifer	Jessica
Anna	Ruth	Jessica	Jennifer
Elizabeth	Helen	Nicole	Stephanie
Emma	Margaret	Melissa	Melissa
Alice	Elizabeth	Michelle	Christina
Edith	Dorothy	Maria	Nicole
May	Catherine	Lisa	Amanda
Helen	Mildred	Elizabeth	Ashley
Katherine	Frances	Danielle	Tiffany
Grace	Alice	Christine	Samantha

Women are less traditional—none of the female names appeared each of the four times.

THE TEN MOST POPULAR SURNAMES IN AMERICA

1. Smith
2. Johnson
3. William (s) (son)
4. Brown
5. Jones
6. Miller
7. Davis
8. Wilson
9. Ander (son) (sen)
10. Taylor

Source: Richard Thomas, *First 300 Years of 2,000 Most Common Surnames in America and Their Frequency* (Salt Lake City, Utah: Accelerated Indexing Systems International, 1989).

MOST COMMON SURNAMES IN TEN AMERICAN CITIES

The following are lists of the most popular last names in ten American cities based on their telephone directories. (Consequently, actual figures might vary slightly when those individuals who may not have telephones are included.) The reason for choosing a cross-section of ten U.S. cities is to demonstrate how surnames vary according to different regions, reflecting the ethnic makeup of these cities.

The Top Ten Most Popular First Names
for Children in the United States

The following are the ten most popular names for girls and boys in the United States in 1988, the lastest list available:

Girls	Boys
Ashley	Michael
Amanda	Matthew
Jessica	Christopher
Nichole	Andrew
Sarah	Joshua
Jennifer	David
Lauren	Daniel
Brittany	Robert
Samantha	John
Stephanie	Justin

Source: *USA Today*, November 29, 1989, section A, page 10.

Greater Atlanta

1. Smith
2. William(s) (son)
3. Johnson
4. Jones
5. Brown(e)

6. Davis
7. Harris(on)
8. Thomas
9. Wilson
10. Jackson

Boston

1. Smith
2. Brown(e)
3. Johnson
4. Kell(e)y
5. Murphy

6. William(s) (son)
7. Cohen (an), etc.
8. Miller
9. Lee
10. White

41

Chicago

1. Johnson	6. Davis
2. William(s) (son)	7. Harris(on)
3. Smith	8. Jackson
4. Jones	9. Miller
5. Brown(e)	10. Anderson

Denver

1. Smith	6. William(s) (son)
2. Johnson	7. Jones
3. Miller	8. Davis
4. Brown(e)	9. Wilson
5. Anderson	10. Peter (s) (son)

Indianapolis

1. Smith	6. Miller
2. Johnson	7. Davis
3. William(s) (son)	8. Wilson
4. Jones	9. Moore
5. Brown(e)	10. Taylor

Los Angeles

1. William(s) (son)	6. Lee
2. Smith	7. Rodriguez
3. Johnson	8. Brown(e)
4. Gonzal(ez) (es)	9. Martinez
5. Garcia	10. Jones

Greater Memphis

1. Smith	6. Davis
2. William(s) (son)	7. Taylor
3. Jones	8. Harris(on)
4. Johnson	9. Allen
5. Brown(e)	10. Moore

Greater Miami

1. Rodriguez
2. Gonzal(ez) (es)
3. Garcia
4. Perez
5. Hernandez
6. Fernandez
7. Martinez
8. Diaz
9. Lopez
10. Smith

Minneapolis

1. Ander (son) (sen)
2. Peters (son) (sen)
3. Olson (sen)
4. Nelson
5. Larson (sen)
6. Smith
7. Miller
8. Carlson (sen)
9. Erickson
10. William(s) (son)

New York (Manhattan)

1. Smith
2. Brown(e)
3. William(s) (son)
4. Cohen (Cohan, etc.)
5. Lee
6. Johnson
7. Rodriguez
8. Green(e)
9. Davis
10. Jones

Interestingly, Denver is most representative of the ten above cities with nine of America's ten most common names. Miami, on the other hand, has only one, Smith.

Most Common Surname in the United States

The most common last name in the English-speaking world is *Smith*. There are an estimated 2,382,509 Smiths in the United States.

Why Do We Give Children the Father's Surname?

Not all cultures trace lineage through the father's family. In Tahiti, for instance, children used to be named after the mother's side of the family. Before the use of established surnames in Western culture, a man had a given name and was also known as somebody's son. The Scandinavians expressed this with the suffix -son, as in Johnson, or John's son. In Scotland a Mac or Mc before the name did the same thing: MacDonald was the son of Donald. In Ireland James, son of Neill, became James O'Neill. These names became fixed when Napoleon demanded that every man have a family name for record-keeping purposes—a patronymic that all his descendents would bear.

Calling all Bobs

Bob Idso of St. Peter, Minnesota, is the founder of *Bobs International*, an organization with one requirement for membership. Only people named *Bob* can join. Formed in 1985, this elite group promotes *Bob* as a marvelous name and Idso insists every Bob should take pride in his or her name. Idso points out that the name is so exceptional that *Bob* is included in many words such as:

Animals	Bobigny, France
Bobcat	Bobingen, Germany
Bobolink	Boboc, Romania
Bobtail nag	Bobo Dioulasso, Upper Volta
Bobwhite	**Bobolice, Poland**
	Bobonong, Botswana
Cities	**Boboshevo, Bulgaria**
Boba, Hungary	**Bobovdol, Bulgaria**
Bobai, China	Bobrka, Russia
Bobbili, India	Bobrov, Russia
Bobcaygeon, Canada	Bobrovichskoye, Russia

Bobrowice, Poland
Bobrowniki, Poland
Bobruysk, Russia
Bobtown, Pennsylvania
Bobures, Venezuela

Islands
Boblo

Protagonists
Bobbsey Twins

Fashion
Bobbed hair
Bobby sox

Sporting Goods
Bobber

Tools
Bobbin
Bobby pin
Plumb bob
Bobstay

Food
Shish kebab

Games
Bobbing for apples
Dancing a Bob

Vehicles
Bobsled

Incidentally, you don't have to be named Bob to visit Idso's famous Bob's Gallery in St. Peter, Minnesota. Everybody is welcome. So from now on, if your name is Bob, be proud. It's a grand old name! For more information, write to: Bobs International, RTE 1, Box 120, St. Peter, MN 56082

The Most Common Last Name in the World

The most common last name in the world is the Chinese name *Chang*. It is estimated that 9.7 percent to 12.1 percent of Chinese people, or at least 104 million people, use that surname. This is more than the entire population of all but seven of the 170 other sovereign countries in the world.

OUR FIFTY STATES

■

When traveling through the states did you ever wonder how they got their names? Well quit wondering and read on!

Alabama. Alabama was named for the great river that runs through the state, called *Alibamon* by the southern Indian tribe whose habitat was in central Alabama. There are many different theories as to what *Alabama* actually means. Depending on the source, Alabama means either "here we rest," "thicket-clearers," "vegetation-gatherers," or "mulberry people."

Alaska. *Alaska* was named after the Aleut word *Alaxsxq,* which means "great land," or from *alakshak,* meaning "peninsula."

Arizona. *Arizona* got its name from the Papago word *arizonac,* meaning "little springs."

Arkansas. *Arkansas* got its name from the Arkansas Indians known as the Quappaw, which means "downstream people."

California. In *Las Sergas de Esplandian* by Garci Ordonez de Montalvo, a queen named Calafia ruled over a fabulous country, hence called *California*. The book was popular with the conquistadors, who first explored this area in the mid 1500s.

Colorado. Colorado got its name from the Colorado River. The sixteenth-century Spanish explorers called the river *Colorado* meaning "red" or "ruddy," because it flows through magnificent ravines of red stone.

Connecticut. *Connecticut* is derived from an Algonquian word, *quinnehtukqut,* meaning "beside the long tidal river."

Delaware. *Delaware* was named after the first governor of Virginia, Thomas West, baron de la Warr, in the early 1600s. When a strong storm forced one of Virginia's ships to seek shelter in what is now known as the Delaware Bay, the captain of the ship named the land at the mouth of the bay Cape La Warr (now Cape Henlopen), and in time, both the bay and the land to the north and west of the bay became known as Delaware.

Florida. Ponce de León named this territory *Florida* after landing there in 1513. The name means "flowery, full of flowers" in Spanish.

Georgia. *Georgia* was named in honor of George II, the king of England. King George granted a charter for the colony on June 9, 1732, to James Edward Oglethorpe and a board of 21 trustees, who established the colony in 1733.

Hawaii. There are several explanations for the origin of the name *Hawaii*. The first is that it was named after Hawaii Loa, traditional discoverer of the Islands. The second is that it was named after the traditional home of the Polynesians, Hawaii or Hawaiki. This compound word comes from *Hawa,* which is the name of the traditional place of resi-

Nebraska. *Nebraska* was named after the Platte River, which the Omaha Indians called *Nibthaska* meaning "flat water."

Nevada. The state was named when the first Spanish explorers saw the snow-capped Sierra Nevada mountains in the sixteenth century. *Nevada* is a Spanish word meaning "snow-clad" or "snow-capped," and *Sierra* means "maintains."

New Hampshire. John Mason, the largest landholder in the region, named *New Hampshire* in the 1600s for Hampshire, his home county in England.

New Jersey. Sir George Carteret, one of the landowners of *New Jersey*, named the land in the 1660s after his birthplace, the island of Jersey in the English Channel off the coast of France.

New Mexico. *New Mexico* got its name with the signing of the Treaty of Cordova on August 24, 1821. The Spanish-American colonies secured their independence from Spain, and New Mexico became a part of the Mexican Republic. The name may derive from the name of the Aztec god of war, Mixitli.

New York. The former Dutch colony New Amsterdam was renamed in 1664 after an English fleet sailed into the harbor and forced Governor Peter Stuyvesant to surrender. The English colony was then named New York in honor of the duke of York, who became King James II.

North Carolina. This state was originally named *Carolana,* which is a Latin form of "Charles" I of England, in 1629. In 1663, Charles II renamed it Carolina.

North Dakota. *North Dakota* got its name from the Dakota Indians, the first inhabitants of the area. Congress named it the Dakota Territory in 1881. In the Siouan language, the name *Dakota* means "allies," and was used to refer to the confederacy of Sioux tribes.

Ohio. *Ohio* was named for the Ohio River. The Iroquoian word means "something big," like the Ohio River, which was also called "The Great River" or "beautiful river."

Oklahoma. *Oklahoma* got its name from two Choctaw Indian words: *okla,* which means "people" and *homa,* which means "red."

Oregon. *Oregon* was named after the River of the West, also called the Oregon. In 1778, explorer Jonathan Carver published an account of his travels in the West and used the word *Oregon* to describe the river. It may come from the Indian word *ouragan,* meaning "birch-bark dish."

Pennsylvania. This state was named after the father of its seventeenth-century founder, William Penn. *Sylvania* is Latin for "wooded land," hence "Penn's woods."

Rhode Island. Rhode Island may have been named for the Greek island of Rhodes. Its original name was "State of Rhode Island and Providence Plantations," the name for Providence and other towns on the mainland.

South Carolina. Like North Carolina, *South Carolina* was named after King Charles I of England. It was originally called *Carolana,* a Latin variant of the king's name.

South Dakota. *South Dakota* was named after the Dakota Indians, the first inhabitants of the territory. The Indians called themselves *Dakota,* which means "allies."

Tennessee. This state was named for the Tennessee River, which is derived from the Indian word *Tenasee,* the name of a Cherokee village near the river. The name may mean "bend in the river."

Texas. *Texas* got its name from the Caddo Indian word *tejas,* or *teyas,* meaning "friends" or "allies."

Utah. *Utah* got its name from the first inhabitants of the area, the Ute or Uta, which means "hill dwellers" or "people of the mountain."

Vermont. *Vermont* was named by seventeenth-century French explorers. *Verd mont* (or *vert mont*) means "green mountain."

Virginia. This state was named in the seventeenth century from the Latin *virginius,* in honor of Queen Elizabeth I of England, also known as the Virgin Queen.

Washington. The area now known as *Washington* was named in 1853 after President George Washington. It is the only state named after a president.

West Virginia. This territory was renamed *West Virginia* after it broke away from Virginia at the beginning of the Civil War.

Wisconsin. *Wisconsin* comes from the Menomonee Indian word meaning "wild rushing channel" or "river of a thousand islands." It was called variously *Wiskonsan, Ouiconsin,* and *Misconsing* by early settlers, but became Wisconsin on July 4, 1836.

Wyoming. This state got its name from *Meche-weami-ing,* Delaware Indian words meaning "large plains." J. M. Ashley, representative from Ohio, named the area *Wyoming* in 1865 when introducing a bill to Congress providing a temporary government for the area.

STATE NICKNAMES

■

It's interesting how each state in the Union has at least one nickname. Some are historic while others are hilarious. For example, why is Oklahoma called the *Sooner State,* or Missouri called the *Show Me State?* This chapter looks at the stories behind the most popular state nicknames.

Alabama. Alabama has two popular nicknames. The first one is the *Cotton State* because Alabama is a big cotton-producing area. The second one is the *Yellowhammer State.* This became a nickname during the Civil War because the gray uniforms of the Confederate soldiers had a yellowish tinge since they were hand-dyed.

Alaska. Alaska's nicknames are *America's Ice Box* and *The Frozen Wilderness* because it is partially covered with snow and ice all year-round.

Arizona. Arizona's most popular nickname is the *Grand Canyon State* because the Grand Canyon of the Colorado River is situated mostly in Northern Arizona.

Arkansas. Arkansas is nicknamed the *Land of Opportunity* because of its natural resources, which include its store of mineral wealth and its vast forests of pine and hardwood, and its agricultural and horticultural prowess.

California. California is called the *Golden State* because of the discovery and extensive mining of gold there.

Colorado. Colorado is called the *Centennial State* because the state constitution was adopted in 1876, 100 years after the United States Constitution was adopted.

Connecticut. Connecticut is nicknamed the *Constitution State* and the *Nutmeg State*. It is called the *Constitution State* because in 1639, at Hartford, the Fundamental Orders, which is thought to be the first constitution written in the United States, were drawn up. The Constitution of the United States is said to have been influenced by that of Connecticut. It is also called the *Nutmeg State* because its early inhabitants had the reputation of being so cunning they could sell wooden nutmegs.

Delaware. Delaware is nicknamed the *First State* because it was first to ratify the U.S. Constitution. It is also nicknamed the *Diamond State* because of its small size, and *The Blue Hen State* for its large poultry industry.

Florida. Florida's most popular nicknames are the *Sunshine State* and the *Peninsula State* for obvious reasons.

Georgia. Georgia is nicknamed the *Empire State of the South* because it is the largest state east of the Mississippi. Others call it the *Peach State*, a more popular name that now appears on Georgia license plates. (There is no peach more juicy than a Georgia peach!)

Hawaii. Hawaii is nicknamed the *Aloha State*, which comes from the local word for "love," used to greet someone or say good-bye.

Idaho. Idaho is nicknamed the *Gem State* because of its beautiful mountains. It is also called the *Spud State* because of its numerous potato farms.

Illinois. Illinois is nicknamed the *Prairie State* because of the vast expanse of rolling prairies within the state. It is also called the *Land of Lincoln* because Abraham Lincoln lived most of his life there and was buried in Springfield.

Indiana. There are many explanations for why Indiana is nicknamed the *Hoosier State*. The most common one is that its early settlers always cried out "who's yere?" when someone knocked on their door. Another story is that the original form of the word was *hoozer*, which meant "hill dweller" or "highlander." The most practical explanation is that it is named for Sam Hoosier, a canal builder who employed a lot of workers and were therefore identified as being "Hoosiers."

Iowa. Iowa's most popular nickname is the *Hawkeye State*. There are two different explanations for why it was named this. The first claims it was named for the Indian Chief Hawkeye, who was once the terror of travelers along its border. The second explanation says that the nickname came from J. G. Edwards, also known as "Old Hawkeye." He was the editor of the *Burlington Patriot,* which was later named the *Hawkeye and Patriot.*

Kansas. Kansas is nicknamed the *Sunflower State* for the tall, yellow prairie flowers that thrive throughout the state.

Kentucky. Kentucky is nicknamed the *Bluegrass State* due to its abundant growth of bluegrass in its rich limestone soil.

Louisiana. Louisiana is nicknamed the *Pelican State* because of the pelican in its state coat of arms.

Maine. Maine is nicknamed the *Pine Tree State* because of the white pine that has been one of Maine's greatest assets from its earliest history.

Maryland. Maryland is nicknamed the *Old Line State* after its heroic "troops of the line" during the revolutionary war. It is also called the *Free State* because so many Marylanders wanted local matters to be controlled by local governments.

Massachusetts. Massachusetts is nicknamed the *Bay State* because the Puritans founded their colony on Massachusetts Bay.

Michigan. Michigan's most popular nickname is the *Wolverine State* because of the numerous prairie wolves that abounded there. More recently it has been called the *Auto State* because of its prominence in automobile manufacturing.

Minnesota. Minnesota has been nicknamed the *Land of 10,000 Lakes* for its abundance of lakes (there are actually 22,000).

Mississippi. Mississippi has been nicknamed the *Magnolia State* due to the abundance of magnolia trees throughout the state.

Missouri. Missouri is nicknamed the *Show Me State* because Willard D. Vandiver, a former representative from Missouri to the U.S. Congress, once challenged a colleague's program, saying, "I'm from Missouri, and you've got to show me."

Montana. Montana is called the *Treasure State* because its mountains supplied early settlers with gold and silver.

Nebraska. Nebraska has been nicknamed the *Corn Husker State* because the University of Nebraska football team is called the Corn Huskers. Of course, long before the game of football, Nebraska was known for its reputation as a fertile corn-growing state.

Nevada. Nevada has been called the *Sagebrush State* because of its gray-green sagebrush. It is more commonly known as the *Silver State* because of the vast amounts of silver that came from its mines.

New Hampshire. New Hampshire has been nicknamed the *White Mountain State* and the *Granite State* because of its white mountains in the northern part of the state and its extensive granite quarries.

New Jersey. New Jersey is called the *Garden State* because of its extensive truck farms catering to the New York and Philadelphia metropolitan areas.

New Mexico. New Mexico is called the *Land of Opportunity* because of its natural beauty, ideal climate, and numerous industries. It is also nicknamed the *Sunshine State* because of the high percentage of sunshine it gets and the *Spanish State* for its nearness to Mexico and its large Spanish-speaking population.

New York. New York is known as the *Empire State* because of its commanding position, vast wealth, and enterprise of its people. The name, of course, has become associated with one of the most famous buildings in the world, the Empire State Building.

North Carolina. North Carolina is known as the *Tar Heel State* because of the abundant tar and turpentine industry there. Others say the nickname developed during a battle in the Civil War when Robert E. Lee said to one of his officers, "Look at those North Carolina boys. They're holding their ground like they have tar on their heels."

Ohio. Ohio is known as the *Buckeye State* because of the buckeye trees that grow there.

Oklahoma. Oklahoma is called the *Sooner State* because when the territory of Oklahoma was opened to settlement at a given hour, there were many who did not abide by the law and went before the appointed time to gain an unfair advantage in staking their land claim—they were the "sooners" who arrived too soon.

Oregon. Oregon is nicknamed the *Beaver State* because of the abundance of beavers in earlier times and because of the beaver's association with intelligence, industry, and ingenuity.

Pennsylvania. Pennsylvania is called the *Keystone State* because its name appeared on the thirteenth, or key, stone of the arch of the bridge between the city of Washington and the community of Georgetown. Geographically, Pennsylvania formed the bridge between New England and the Southern colonies. It is nicknamed the *Quaker State* because Pennsylvania was founded by William Penn, who was a Quaker and encouraged Quaker settlement.

Rhode Island. Rhode Island is nicknamed *Little Rhody* because of its size.

South Carolina. South Carolina is nicknamed the *Palmetto State* because of the palmetto tree in the seal of the commonwealth. The palmetto is a common tree in the state.

South Dakota. South Dakota is called the *Coyote State* because there are many coyotes that inhabit the land. Because

South Dakota gets more than its share of sunshine, it is also nicknamed the *Sunshine State.*

Tennessee. Tennessee is called the *Volunteer State* because on May 26, 1847, Governor Aaron V. Brown called for three regiments of soldiers to serve in the Mexican War; 30,000 volunteered at once, hence the nickname.

Texas. Texas is called the *Lone Star State* because of the star in the center of its flag.

Utah. Utah is nicknamed the *Beehive State.* In 1849–50, the Mormons called the region *Deseret,* which means "honey bee" from the *Book of Mormon* (Ether 2:3).

Vermont. Vermont is nicknamed the *Green Mountain State* for the green mountains within its boundary.

Virginia. Virginia is nicknamed the *Old Dominion.* King Charles II named it this because it remained loyal to the Crown during the English Civil War of the mid 1600s.

Washington. Washington is nicknamed the *Chinook State* because it was previously the home of the Lower Chinook branch of North American Indians. It is also called the *Evergreen State* because of its big green firs.

West Virginia. West Virginia is called the *Mountain State* because the Allegheny Mountains cover more than one-third of the state. It is also nicknamed the *Panhandle State* because of its shape.

Wisconsin. Wisconsin is nicknamed the *Badger State* because the early land miners there made homes for themselves by digging into the hillside and living underground just like the badger in his burrow.

Wyoming. Wyoming is nicknamed the *Equality State* because of its early acceptance of women's suffrage.

HOW SOME AMERICAN CITIES WERE NAMED

■

Did you ever wonder how certain cities in the United States got their names? Some people live in a city their entire lives and never know the origin of its name. While the reason some cities, like Columbus, Ohio, were named is obvious, for others, it is not. For instance, how do you think Chicago was named? This chapter tells how many U.S. cities got their names.

Albany. This city was named in the seventeenth century after the duke of York and Albany who later became King James II of England.

Albuquerque. *Albuquerque,* in New Mexico, is derived from the Spanish words *quercus,* which means "oak," and *albus,* which means "white."

Alexandria. This city in Virginia was named after Alexander the Great, who conquered all the known world in the fourth century B.C. The family that owned much of the land in the town was also named Alexander.

Ann Arbor. *Ann Arbor* was named because two of its early settlers had wives named Ann, and the land was a pretty grove, that is "an arbor."

Atlanta. *Atlanta* was so named by its proud inhabitants to show that they were connected with the Atlantic Ocean by the Western and Atlantic Railroad when the city was incorporated in 1847.

Auburn. This city in New York got its name from a line in the poem "The Deserted Village" by eighteenth-century British poet, Oliver Goldsmith. In the poem, Goldsmith writes of "Sweet Auburn, loveliest village of the plain."

Austin. *Austin,* Texas, was named after Stephen F. Austin, who established the first permanent American colony in Texas in 1822.

Baltimore. *Baltimore* was named after George Calvert, Lord Baltimore, to whom Maryland was granted in 1632. Lord Baltimore's title is derived from the Celtic words *baile-an-tighe-mhoir,* meaning "town of the great house."

Baton Rouge. *Baton Rouge,* meaning "red staff," was named by the French who claimed Louisiana in the late seventeenth century. There are two theories about why it was given this name. The first is that a great, red cypress tree marked the boundary between the territories of the French settlers and the Indians. The second is that this is where Indians supposedly first massacred the settlers.

Berkeley. *Berkeley,* California, was named after Bishop George Berkeley, who founded the college there in about 1730.

Bethlehem. *Bethlehem,* Pennsylvania, was named on Christmas Day in 1741, after the birthplace of Jesus Christ. In Hebrew, *beth* is "house" and *lechem* means "bread," thus "bread house."

Billings. *Billings,* Montana, was named in the nineteenth century after the president of the Northern Pacific Railroad, F. Billings.

Birmingham. Like many American cities named by British forebears, *Birmingham,* Alabama, was named after the city in England. It comes from the ham, or "home" of the "Boerings."

Bismarck. This city in North Dakota was named for the nineteenth-century German chancellor, Otto von Bismarck, after German investors provided funds for the local railroad. *Bismarck* means "the bishop's land."

Bloomington. Bloomington, home of Indiana University, was named in the early 1800s after William Bloom, an early settler.

Boise. *Boise,* Idaho, was named for the French word *boise,* meaning "woody." It was so named because there were numerous trees along the Boise River.

Boston. *Boston* was named by the colonists in the seventeenth century for their hometown in England.

Bridgeport. This Connecticut city got its name because of the bridge across the Pequonnock River at the harbor. Many other cities have the same name for a similar reason.

Buffalo. The origin of *Buffalo*'s name is quite obvious. It was named in 1801 because buffalo were still found this far east. According to another story, the city was named after a Seneca Indian whose name translates to "Buffalo."

Burlington. *Burlington* got its name from a family in New York. The name was made up of the Anglo-Saxon words *bur*, meaning "a storehouse," and *tun*, meaning "a farmyard enclosure."

Cambridge. *Cambridge*, Massachusetts, was named in the seventeenth century for the city in England.

Cedar Rapids. The origin of the name *Cedar Rapids* is obvious, referring to the trees along the Cedar River and the rapids near where the city is located.

Charleston. Like the state itself, *Charleston*, South Carolina, was named after Charles II of England by the early colonists.

Charlotte. *Charlotte*, North Carolina, was named after Queen Charlotte, the wife of George III of England.

Charlottesville. Charlottesville, Virginia, was also named after Queen Charlotte, the wife of England's George III.

Cheyenne. The name *Cheyenne* is from the Dakota Indian word *šahíyena*, meaning "people of a foreign language." The Indians of Cheyenne were named this by their neighbors in what is now Wyoming.

Chicago. *Chicago* is derived from an Algonquian Indian name, *she-kag-ong*, meaning "place of the wild onions."

Cincinnati. *Cincinnati* took its name from the Society of the Cincinnati, an organization of officers who had fought in the Revolutionary War. They named themselves after Cincinnatus, a Roman Patriot in the fifth century B.C. who led his country in time of need, just as these men did during the war.

66

Cleveland. This city was named after Gen. Moses Cleveland, who mapped its site in 1796.

Columbus. *Columbus,* Ohio, was named after fifteenth-century explorer Christopher Columbus. While there are several cities in the United States named after the discoverer, the Ohio capital is the largest in the world bearing his name.

Dayton. In 1796, *Dayton,* Ohio, was named for one of its first landowners, Jonathan Dayton.

Denver. *Denver* was named in 1858 after the governor of Kansas, James W. Denver. At that time, Colorado was part of Kansas.

Des Moines. This Iowa city was first called an Indian name, *moingona,* meaning "a place on the road." It was later shortened to *moin* by the French, who called the river *Riviere des Moins,* or "river of the road." Years later, the Indian origin of *moins* was forgotten, and the words were written *Riviere des Moines,* which meant "river of the monks."

Detroit. *Detroit* is a French word that means "strait" or "narrow." The name was first applied to the Detroit River, and later to the city.

Dubuque. Dubuque, Iowa, was named after its eighteenth-century founder, Julien Dubuque, a French trader and miner.

El Paso. *El Paso* means "the pass" or "the gap" in Spanish and refers to the canyon cut by the Rio Grande in west Texas.

Eugene. *Eugene,* Oregon, was named in 1851 for one of its first settlers, Eugene F. Skinner.

Flint. The name of this Michigan city is the English translation of *pawonnuk-ening,* an Indian word meaning "the river of flint."

Fort Worth. *Fort Worth,* Texas, was named after General William J. Worth, who fought in the Mexican War in the 1840s.

Hampton. The name of Hampton, Virginia, was derived from the Indian word *huntenatun,* which means "the camp of the huntsmen."

Harrisburg. The capital of Pennsylvania was named after John Harris, a storekeeper who founded the city in 1785.

Houston. *Houston* was named after Gen. Sam Houston, who won the independence of the Republic of Texas from Mexico in the Battle of San Jacinto in 1836. The name *Houston* may be derived from "Hugh's Town" in England.

Jacksonville. Along with Jackson, Michigan, and Jackson, Mississippi, Jacksonville, Florida, was named after the seventh president of the United States, Andrew Jackson (1767–1845). Jacksonville was originally named Fort St. Nicholas by the Spanish in 1740 and renamed in honor of the president during his term (1829–1837).

Kalamazoo. *Kalamazoo* started off as *negikanamazo,* an Ojibwa word meaning "otter tail."

Knoxville. Knoxville, Tennessee, was named after the revolutionary war soldier Henry Knox (1750–1806).

Joe, Montana

Quarterback great Joe Montana, who starred for the San Francisco 49ers for many years and then signed with the Kansas City Chiefs, is now immortalized more than 1,000 miles west of his team's hometown. The citizens of Ismay, Montana, voted to change the town's name to *Joe*. That's right, *Joe, Montana*. The name change began on July 3, 1993; every year between the months of July and the month the Super Bowl is played, all signs located at the city limits will read: Welcome to Joe, Montana. In the off-season, the name changes back once again to Ismay. Joe, Montana, population 22, has a grain elevator, a fire department, two council members, and a mayor. It occupies four acres of land.

One other American athlete who had a town named after him comes to mind. There's a town called Jim Thorpe, Pennsylvania, named after the legendary Native American superstar.

Laramie. Laramie, Wyoming, was named after a French fur trader and explorer, Jacques Laramie, who died in 1821.

Lincoln. This Nebraska city was named after the sixteenth U.S. president, Abraham Lincoln (1809–1865).

Los Angeles. *Los Angeles* is a shortened version of *Reina de los Angeles,* or "queen of the angels," in Spanish. Originally called San Gabriel, the pueblo was established by Spanish explorers in 1771.

Louisville. *Louisville,* Kentucky, was named after King Louis XVI of France by settlers in 1778 because of his country's help in the American Revolution.

Lynchburg. This city in Virginia was named after its founder, John Lynch.

Madison. *Madison,* Wisconsin, was named after James Madison (1751–1836), the fourth president of the United States.

Manchester. *Manchester,* New Hampshire, was named for the city of the same name in England. The name was originally the Celtic *Mancenion,* whereby *man* meant "place" and *cenion* meant "skins," that is, "the place where the skins were traded." It was later changed to *Manceaster* before being called its present name.

Memphis. *Memphis,* Tennessee, was named after Memphis, once a capital of ancient Egypt on the Nile. It is the Greek derivation of the Egyptian term *ma-m-phtah,* which meant the "place of Phtah." Phtah was the god of fire.

Milwaukee. The name *Milwaukee* is the English version of the Algonquian Indian word *miloaki,* which means "good land" or "council place."

Montgomery. This city in Alabama was named after Gen. Richard Montgomery, the revolutionary war soldier who was killed in 1775 in an attack on Quebec.

Nantucket. *Nantucket,* Massachusetts, is an Indian tribe's name that means "its sterile soil tempts no one."

Nashville. In 1794, *Nashville,* Tennessee, was named after General Francis Nash, a revolutionary war hero.

New Orleans. This city was named *Nouvelle Orléans* by French settlers in 1718 in honor of Philippe II, the duke of Orléans. Also the name of a French city, *Orléans* is derived from the Latin *Civitas Aurelianorum,* "city of the Emperor Aurelian."

Newark. *Newark* was named for an English city where some of its colonists came from. The city was the "new work" or castle.

Newport. *Newport*, Rhode Island, got its name when settlers from Boston established a new harbor (new port).

Olympia. *Olympia*, Washington, was named after the Greek Mt. Olympus on which the gods were thought to dwell. The word means "shining heights" in Greek.

Omaha. *Omaha* comes from a Siouan Indian word that means "upstream people."

Palo Alto. The name *Palo Alto*, in California, literally means "tall log" in Spanish, probably a reference to the majestic redwoods Spanish explorers found there in the eighteenth century.

Pasadena. The name of this California city is derived from the Ojibwa *pasadinaa*, meaning "crown of the valley."

Pensacola. This city in Florida takes its name from the Indian *pan-sha-okla*, which means "hairy people."

Philadelphia. In 1682 founder William Penn named this settlement after the city of Philadelphos in Greece. The Greek *philadelphia* means "brotherly love."

Phoenix. *Phoenix* is named for the mythical bird of Arabia. As the story goes, the bird lives for 500 or 600 years, burns itself to ashes in a huge bonfire, and then rises from the flames to live another 500 years. The city in Arizona was built on the prehistoric ruins of an ancient Hohokam Indian city.

71

Pittsburgh. George Washington named this city after William Pitt, the prime minister of Great Britain and a leader of the Seven Years' War against France in the mid-1700s.

Plymouth. *Plymouth,* Massachusetts, was named after the seaport on the River Plym in England from which the Pilgrims set sail for the New World in the *Mayflower* on September 6, 1620.

Portland. *Portland,* Oregon, was named after the Maine hometown of one of its first settlers.

Prescott. *Prescott,* Arizona, was named after the historian William H. Prescott, who recorded the events of the Spanish conquests in the New World.

Providence. This city in Rhode Island was named by Roger Williams in gratitude "for God's merciful providence to me in my distress." Williams left the Massachusetts Bay colony rather than give up his religious beliefs.

Pueblo. *Pueblo,* Colorado, was named after the Mexican city *Puebla de los Angeles. Pueblo* in Spanish means "village."

Raleigh. *Raleigh,* North Carolina, was named after the explorer Sir Walter Raleigh, who sponsored the ill-fated expedition that colonized Roanoke Island off the coast of North Carolina in 1587.

Reno. *Reno,* Nevada, was named after the Union Gen. Jesse L. Reno.

Richmond. *Richmond,* Virginia, was named in the early seventeenth century in honor of the son of Charles II of England, the duke of Richmond. The name *Richmond* comes

Most Popular Names for Towns

The following names of towns are the most common in the
United States:

Franklin (28); after statesman Benjamin Franklin
Madison (27); after President James Madison
Clinton (26); personal name, now a U.S. President
Washington (26); after President George Washington
Chester (25); town in England
Greenville (24); description
Marion (24); revolutionary war general
Salem (24); biblical place
Springfield (24); description
Manchester (23); English city
Monroe (22); after President James Monroe
Troy (22); literature, history
Ashland (21); tree; home of Henry Clay
Milford (21); English town, ford near a mill
Clayton (20); description, personal name
Fairfield (20); description
Jackson (20); after President Andrew Jackson
Jamestown (20); English king, personal name
Jefferson (20); after President Thomas Jefferson
Newport (20); description
Oxford (20); English city
Cleveland (19); after President Grover Cleveland
Lebanon (19); biblical place
Plymouth (19); English city

from the French *rich-mont*, which means "rich" or "fertile mountain."

Roanoke. *Roanoke* comes from the Indian word *rarenawok*, which means "smoothed shells." The Indians used it for money. Roanoke Island was the site of two abortive colonies off the coast of North Carolina. The colonists in the first expedition returned to England in 1586. More than 100 people who established a second colony in 1587 disappeared.

Rochester. *Rochester,* New York, was named after the original proprietor Col. Nathaniel Rochester, a revolutionary war officer. The name *Rochester* originated in England with a man named Hfrofes who founded a ceaster, or settlement. Hfrofes-ceaster eventually became Rochester.

Salem. The name *Salem,* of both Massachusetts and Oregon, is derived from the Hebrew *shalom,* which means "peace." The name appears in the book of Genesis.

San Antonio. Spanish soldiers arrived on the site of what is now *San Antonio* on June 13, 1691, the feast day of St. Anthony of Padua. The city was officially named, however, when the San Antonio de Valero Mission, now called the Alamo, was built in 1718.

San Diego. In 1769 *San Diego* was named by Spanish explorers after San Diego de Alcala, a fifteenth-century Spanish friar. Before this the Spanish had called the site San Miguel.

San Francisco. *San Francisco,* which was explored by the Spanish in 1776, was named after Saint Francis of Assisi.

Santa Fe. The name of this city in New Mexico means "holy faith" in Spanish. A mission was founded here by Spanish explorer Juan de Oñate in 1609.

What the Names of Big Cities Around the World Mean

You learned about how U.S. cities got their names. Now here's what the names of some of the great cities around the world mean:

Amsterdam (Netherlands): "dam on the River Amstel"
Athens (Greece): after Athene, "queen of heaven"
Baghdad (Iraq): "God's gift"
Bermudas (Atlantic islands): after Juan Bermudez, the Spanish explorer
Brisbane (Australia): after Sir Thomas Brisbane, the founder
Brussels (Belgium): "buildings on a marsh"
Buenos Aires (Argentina): "good winds"
Cairo (Egypt): "victorious," part of full Arabic name "Mars the victorious," Mars being visible when the city was founded
Copenhagen (Denmark): "merchants' harbor"
Edmonton (Canada): derived from Edmonton, London; "Eadhelm's estate"
Jamaica (Caribbean island): "island of springs"
Liverpool (England): "pool with clotted water"
Madrid (Spain): "timber"
Melbourne (Australia): after Lord Melbourne, British prime minister
Moscow (Russia): from River Moskva
Ontario (Canada): "beautiful (lake)"
Peking (China): "northern capital"
Quebec (Canada): "place where the river narrows"
Rome (Italy): from River Ruma
Seville (Spain): "lower land"
Tokyo (Japan): "eastern capital"
Vienna (Austria): from River Vienna
Winnipeg (Canada): "muddy water"
Yukon (Canada): from River Yukon, "big river"

Savannah. The name of this city in Georgia is derived from the Indian word *shawano,* which means "the southerners."

Seattle. Founded in 1852 by a band of 21 New England settlers, *Seattle,* was named after an Indian chief, *Se-a-thl.*

Spokane. *Spokane,* Washington, was named for the fabulous sunny weather the area usually gets. *Spokane,* from the Salish Indian word *spokanee,* actually means "children of the sun."

St. Louis. This city, established by French explorers in the early 1700s, was named after Louis IX of France, who had been canonized (declared an officially recognized saint) in 1297.

St. Paul. Once known as *Innijiska,* or the "white rock," this site in Minnesota was the camping ground for Indian tribes. In 1820, Fort Snelling was built to protect the American Fur Company. In 1841, Father Lucian Galtier constructed a small log chapel nearby and dedicated it to Saint Paul. For a while it was called St. Paul's Landing, which was later shortened to St. Paul.

Stockton. This California city was named after Commodore Robert F. Stockton, who was the commander in chief of the Pacific squadron during the Mexican War in the mid-1840s.

Syracuse. *Syracuse,* New York, got its name from a Phoenician city in Sicily. The name was derived from the Phoenician verb *serach,* which means "to stink." The ancient city was located near a bad-smelling swamp.

Tallahassee. The name of this Florida city is from the Creek Indian words *talua,* which means "village," and *hasi,* which

---

Small Towns Named After Big Cities

Many times, settlers lacked the imagination to come up with a new name for a new town—so they adopted the name of a larger city. The following list illustrates how many times the name of a town has been used:

Dayton, Ohio (17)	Newark, N.J. (9)
Buffalo, N.Y. (16)	Louisville, Ky. (9)
Columbus, Ohio (16)	Boston, Mass. (8)
Oakland, Calif. (16)	Dallas, Tex. (8)
Rochester, N.Y. (13)	Houston, Tex. (8)
Portland, Oreg. (12)	Akron, Ohio (7)
Atlanta, Ga. (11)	Miami, Fla. (7)
Denver, Colo. (10)	St. Paul, Minn. (7)

---

means "old." It was so named because it was a very old settlement before the Europeans arrived. *Tallahassee* was founded in the winter of 1539–1540 by Hernando de Soto.

Tampa. *Tampa,* Florida, got its name from the Calusa Indian word *itimpi,* which means "close by" or "near it." Tampa was settled in 1822 and incorporated in 1835.

Terre Haute. The name of this city in Indiana has a French origin—*terre,* meaning "land," and *haute,* meaning "high." Founded by French explorers, it was built on a bank that rises 60 feet above the Wabash River.

Toledo. This Ohio city was named after Toledo, Spain, which was called Toletum in Roman days.

Topeka. The name *Topeka* is probably derived from the Kansa Indian word *toppik'e,* meaning "potato."

Trenton. *Trenton,* New Jersey, was named after Col. William Trent, speaker of the New Jersey House of Assembly in 1720.

Tulsa. Like Tallahassee, this city in Oklahoma got its name from the Creek Indian words *talua,* which means "village," and *hasi,* which means "old," hence "old village."

Tucson. The name *Tucson* is derived from the Piman Indian word *tu-uk-so-on,* which means "black creek."

Wheeling. *Wheeling,* West Virginia, is derived from the Delaware Indian word *whilink,* which means "at the head of the river."

Wichita. *Wichita,* Kansas, got its name from the Caddo Indian tribe of the same name, which sought refuge there during the Civil War.

Winston-Salem. This city in North Carolina was given the name *Winston* for Joseph Winston, a revolutionary war soldier, and the biblical name *Salem* because the group of religious people who first settled there hoped to live in peaceful security.

City Nicknames

■

Every major U.S. city has at least one nickname. For instance, Chicago is called the *Windy City,* and New York City the *Big Apple.* Did you ever wonder where these names originated? You'll find out in this chapter. (Chicago's nickname has nothing to do with the weather.)

Atlanta. Atlanta, Georgia, is nicknamed the *Gate City* or the *Gate City of the South* because much of the South's commerce passes through here. It is also called the *Industrial Metropolis of the Southeast* because of its numerous industrial and manufacturing sites, and *Dogwood City* because of the abundance of dogwood blossoms throughout the city in the spring.

Baltimore. Baltimore, Maryland, is nicknamed *Monument City* because of the large number of monuments found there.

Boston. Boston, Massachusetts, has several nicknames. It is called the *Athens of America* because of its prominence as an educational and literary center similar to Athens, Greece. It is also called the *Puritan City* because of its early settlers, the *Metropolis of New England* because it is the largest city in New England, and *Bean Town* after the famous local dish.

Buffalo. Buffalo, New York, is called the *Bison City* because of the once-abundant herds of North American buffalo. It is also known as the *Queen of the Lakes* and *Queen City of the Lakes* because of its location on the most eastern edge of the Great Lakes. Buffalo is also known as the *Flour City* due to its being one of the nation's largest flour-producing areas.

Charleston. Charleston, South Carolina, is nicknamed *America's Most Historic City* due to its numerous historic buildings and traditions. It is also called the *Palmetto City* because of its abundance of palmetto trees.

Charlotte. Charlotte, North Carolina, was nicknamed the *Hornets Nest* in 1780 by General Charles Cornwallis, the head of the British army, because Charlotte's citizens showed such opposition to the British. Since Charlotte was also the center of opposition to the northern forces during the Civil War, it later adopted a *hornets' nest* as its emblem.

Chattanooga. Chattanooga, Tennessee, is often called the *Gate City* because its location makes it the gateway for commerce between Georgia, Alabama, and Tennessee. It also serves as the route for much of the trade from the east through the south into Mexico.

Cincinnati. Cincinnati, Ohio, is nicknamed *Queen City* and the *Queen City of the South* because of its beautiful surroundings and bright future.

Cleveland. Cleveland, Ohio, is known as the *Forest City* because of its abundant shade trees.

Dallas. Dallas, Texas, is often called the *City of Homes* because of the extravagant houses in the area. It is also called the *Metropolis of the North* because it is the hub of civic,

---

Chicago: *The Windy City*

Although many tourists swear the Chicago winds are the worst anywhere, the city got its nickname the *Windy City* because of its proverbially long-winded politicians, not its weather. In fact, despite Chicago's blustery reputation, it is not among the country's *twelve* windiest cities, according to the National Climatic Center of the United States Weather Bureau, which ranks the leaders as follows:

		Average Wind Speed (mph)
1.	Great Falls, Mont.	13.1
2.	Oklahoma City, Okla.	13.0
3.	Boston, Mass.	12.9
4.	Cheyenne, Wyo.	12.8
5.	Wichita, Kans.	12.7
6.	Buffalo, N.Y.	12.4
7.	Milwaukee, Wis.	11.8
8.	Des Moines, Iowa	11.2
9.	Providence, R.I.	10.9
	Cleveland, Ohio	10.9
	Dallas, Tex.	10.9
	Omaha, Nebr.	10.9

By comparison, Chicago is an oasis of calm, ranking sixteenth, with an average wind speed of only 10.4 miles per hour.

---

religious, educational, and financial activities of north Texas.

Dayton. Dayton, Ohio, is called the *Birthplace of Aviation* because it was the home of Wilbur and Orville Wright.

Denver. Denver, Colorado, is called the *Queen City of the Plains* and the *City of the Plains* because it is on the edge of the Great Plains and was a center of gold mining. It is also called *Convention City* because of all the conventions that are held there due to its pleasant climate and scenic surroundings. However, Denver is best known as the *Mile High City,* acknowledging its elevation at 5,200 feet above sea level.

Des Moines. Des Moines, Iowa, is often called the *Hartford of the West* because it is an insurance center like Hartford, Connecticut. Many insurance companies are domiciled in Des Moines.

Detroit. Detroit, Michigan, is nicknamed the *Motor City* because of the numerous automobile manufacturers located there. Another nickname is *Motown,* short for motor town.

Houston. Houston, Texas, is nicknamed the *City That Built its Seaport* because its 50-mile ship canal stretches to Galveston for easy access to the gulf. It is also called the *Magnolia City* for the abundant magnolia trees there.

Indianapolis. Indianapolis, Indiana, is nicknamed the *Railroad City* because of all the railroad lines that converge there.

Kalamazoo. Kalamazoo, Michigan, is known as the *Celery City* because one of its chief products is celery.

Kansas City. Kansas City, Missouri, is nicknamed the *Heart of America* because of its location near the center of the United States.

Los Angeles. Los Angeles, California, is called the *City of Flowers and Sunshine* because of its sunny weather and the abundance of flowers in its parks and gardens. Of course, for obvious reasons, the nickname *City of Angels* needs no explanation.

Louisville. Louisville, Kentucky, has been called the *City of Beautiful Churches* because of its hundreds of magnificent churches. It is also called *Falls City* because of its location on the Ohio River at its falls or rapids. *Gateway to the South* is its most fitting nickname because its location divides the North from the South.

Madison. Madison, Wisconsin, is nicknamed the *Four Lake City* because it is located near Lakes Kegonsa, Waubesa, Monona, and Mendota.

Memphis. Memphis, Tennessee, is nicknamed *Bluff City* because it is located on the historic Chicksaw Bluff overlooking the Mississippi River.

Miami. Miami, Florida, is called the *Wonder City* and the *Magic City* because of the huge growth in population and property value since its incorporation in 1896.

Milwaukee. Milwaukee, Wisconsin, has been called *Cream City, Cream White City of the Unsalted Seas,* and *Fair White City* because its buildings are made of cream colored bricks from the native clay. It is also called *Milwaukee the Beautiful* because of its location above the stunning Lake Michigan.

Minneapolis. Minneapolis, Minnesota, is known as the *Flour City* because it is one of the greatest flour-producing centers in the United States. It is also nicknamed the *Gateway City* for its location at the head of the Mississippi River and its numerous railroad, bus, and truck lines.

Nashville. Nashville, Tennessee, is known as the *Athens of the South* because of its many educational institutions and buildings in the Greek classical style. It is also called the *Music City* because it has become a recording and broadcasting center for country music.

New Haven. New Haven, Connecticut, is nicknamed the *City of Elms* or *Elm City* because of its vast number of elm trees.

New Orleans. New Orleans, Louisiana, is often termed *Old French Town* because it was under French control during the eighteenth century and still has much French influence. It is also called the *Key of the Great Valley*, the *Great South Gate*, and *Queen of the South* because of its commanding position at the mouth of the Mississippi River. A more recent popular name is the *Big Easy*, in reference to its jazz musicians.

Newport. Newport, Rhode Island, is called the *Capital of Vacation Land* due to its location, climate, beaches, and crowds who vacation there in the summer. It is also called the *Queen of Summer Resorts* because it is easily accessible to the large eastern cities.

New York City. Our nation's biggest city has many nicknames, the two most popular being *Gotham* and *The Big Apple*. Gotham is a village in Nottinghamshire, England. According to legend, in order to prevent King John from establishing a residence nearby—which they feared would raise their taxes—all of the Gothamites feigned madness. The King's messenger's found some of them trying to confine a cuckoo within a bush by joining hands around it, others attaching a cart to a barn to shade the shingles, still others trying to drown eels, etc. The King's advance agents told him upon their return that there was no use settling in a village of fools. It was Washington Irving who first called New York City Gotham, as a satire upon its citizens.

84

The name stuck, but as a synonym rather than a pejorative term.

More recently, according to the New York Convention and Visitors Bureau, New York City's image had fallen to its lowest by 1971: its negative nicknames included "Crime City" and "Fear City." "The Big Apple" is a deliberate attempt by the Bureau to create for New York City an image "with pleasant, positive connotations . . . a bright and shining image." But the Bureau did not invent the term. It originated in the twentieth century among jazz musicians. They had a saying: "There are many apples on the tree, but to play in New York City is to play The Big Time . . . The Big Apple!"

Philadelphia. Philadelphia, Pennsylvania, is nicknamed *American Liberty* because it is the location of Independence Hall, the site of the revolutionary congress and the signing of the Declaration of Independence. It is also called the *Quaker City* after its Quaker founder William Penn. And, of course, it is most commonly referred to as the *City of Brotherly Love.*

Pittsburgh. Pittsburgh, Pennsylvania, is nicknamed the *Steel City* and *Iron City* because it is one of the greatest iron- and steel-manufacturing cities in the world.

Portland. Portland, Maine, is called *Forest City, Beautiful City by the Sea,* and *Hill City* for its great amount of trees and its location on the hilly peninsula on the sea.

Providence. Providence, Rhode Island, is known as the *Beehive of Industry* because of all the commercial ventures established there. It is also called the *Roger Williams City* after its founder and the *Southern Gateway of New England* due to its location in the southern part of the New England states and its harbor on the Providence River.

Sacramento. Sacramento, California, is called *Camellia City* for its abundance of camellia bushes. More than a million bushes, some of them tree-sized, dot the city. Sacramento is also nicknamed *River City* for the Sacramento and American rivers that flow through the city.

San Antonio. San Antonio, Texas, is nicknamed the *Alamo City* because it is the location of the historic battle of the Alamo of 1836. It is also called the *Mission City* because of its old Spanish missions, many of which are still standing.

San Diego. San Diego, California, is called the *Jewel City of California* because of its outstanding mild climate and resort attractions. It is also called *Plymouth of the West* and *Birthplace of California* because it was one of the first settlements to be made on the west coast. Another nickname is *America's Finer City*, a reference made to its fine climate.

San Francisco. San Francisco, California, is nicknamed the *Golden Gate City* for the strait that connects the Pacific Ocean with the San Francisco Bay. San Francisco is also called the *Queen of the Pacific* because it is a gateway to the sea.

Santa Fe. Santa Fe, New Mexico, is often called the *Lone Star of Civilization* because the Mexican settlers in the Rio Grande Valley claimed it was the only town "in a million square miles of lonely desert, mountains, and plain" for a century or more.

Savannah. Savannah, Georgia, is called the *Forest City of the South* because of the vast amount of parks and magnificent shade trees. It is also called the *Garden City* because of its numerous well-kept parks.

St. Louis. St. Louis, Missouri, is called the *Great River City* because it lies on the largest river in America, the Mississippi River.

St. Paul. St. Paul, Minnesota, is called the *Gateway to the Northwest* because it is located near the head of the Mississippi River and is a commercial, industrial, and transportation center. It is also called the *Northstar City* because it is the capital of Minnesota, which is the North Star State.

Toledo. Toledo, Ohio, is known as the *Corn City* because of its location on the Maumee River, which makes it easily accessible to ship large quantities of wheat, corn, and other grains.

Tulsa. Tulsa, Oklahoma, is called the *Oil Capital of the World* because of its huge oil industry and its position as the hub of pipelines that carry natural gas to cities in the northern and eastern United States.

Washington, D.C. Washington, D.C., is most often called the *Capital City* for its location as the capital of the United States.

Cities Nicknamed for Their Local Industry

Akron, Ohio	*Rubber City*
Allentown, Pa.	*Cement City*
Annapolis, Md.	*Crabtown*
Chicago, Ill.	*Hog Butcher for the World*
Kalamazoo, Mich.	*Celery City*
Les Allemands, La.	*Catfish Capital of the World*
Rochester, N.Y.	*Snapshot City*
Sacramento, Calif.	*Almond Capital of the World*
Waterbury, Conn.	*Brass City*
Wheeling, W. Va.	*Nail City*
Yakima, Wash.	*Fruitbowl of the Nation*

Unusual Place Names

■

Have you ever wondered how certain towns in the United States got named? For instance, what are the stories behind the naming of *Climax, Minnesota,* or *Midnight, Mississippi?* If the reasons for naming these towns seem ludicrous—that's because they are!

Accident, Maryland. This town got its name in the mid-eighteenth century. King George of England granted a man named George Deakins about 600 acres of land in payment of a debt. Deakins sent his own group of surveyors to select the best land they could. Coincidentally, King George sent his surveyors to the same piece of land. Deakins named it the "Accidental Tract," which is now called *Accident.*

Bad Axe, Michigan. This town got its name in 1861 when George Willis Pack and Rudolph Papst set out to lay a new state road from the shores of Lake Huron to Bay City. They would stop at each campsite on the way, survey the land for a few days, and choose a name for the area. They named this particular spot *Bad Axe* because when Papst was out searching for firewood he stumbled upon an old, beat-up axe left behind by past campers.

More Colorful Town Names

Here's a list of other towns in the United States that, from the sound of them, must also have a colorful story behind how they were named:

Alligator, Mississippi
Bowlegs, Oklahoma
Broken Arrow, Oklahoma
Bullfrog, Utah
Businessburg, Ohio
Coolville, Ohio
Crooked Creek, Alaska
Cut and Shoot, Texas
Dog Bone, West Virginia
Dogpatch, Arkansas
Good Times, South Carolina
Greasy Ridge, Ohio
Hell, Michigan
Hellgate, Montana and New York
Intercourse, Pennsylvania
Long Bottom, Ohio
Luck, Wisconsin
Luckey, Ohio
Miracle, Kentucky
Nameless, North Dakota
New Deals, Texas

Nice, California
Normal, Alabama and Illinois
Odd, West Virginia
Okay, Oklahoma
Ordinary, Virginia
Paint Lick, Kentucky
Peoples, Kentucky
Rich, Mississippi
Santa Claus, Indiana
Shickshinny, Pennsylvania
Smartt, Tennessee
Story, Arkansas and Wyoming
Temperanceville, Virginia
Troublesome, Colorado
Tie Siding, Wyoming
Upper Black Eddy, Pennsylvania
What Cheer, Iowa
Whipple, Ohio
Why, Arizona
Whynot, North Carolina
Zap, North Dakota

Bird in Hand, Pennsylvania. This town was named after an old tavern that originally stood there.

Brothers, Oregon, and Sisters, Oregon. Pioneers who settled at the edge of both the Willamette and the Deschutes national forests named their town *Sisters* in 1810 after three nearby mountain peaks Faith, Hope, and Charity. *Brothers* was named 30 years later because a family with six sons settled this land near *Sisters.*

Busy, Kentucky. This town was named in 1929 by its citizens, who made numerous submissions to name the small community around the new post office. *Busy* was chosen because the post office workers said they were too busy to check if any of the submissions were already used as city names in Kentucky.

Cape Fear, North Carolina. This name was chosen in 1585 by an English explorer who nearly wrecked his ship here.

Captain Cook, Hawaii. This Hawaiian town was named after British navy Captain James Cook. After numerous voyages in the Pacific, Cook and his crew would migrate to the Hawaiian Islands during the winter to escape the cold. The islanders admired his feats and the priests proclaimed him a god in 1779. They named the town *Captain Cook* in his honor.

Towns That Are Palindromes*

Ada, Kansas (also Michigan, Minnesota, Ohio, and Oklahoma)
Ama, Louisiana
Anna, Illinois (also Ohio and Texas)
Ava, Illinois (also Missouri, New York, and Ohio)
Ono, California (also Pennsylvania)
Oto, Iowa
Pep, New Mexico (also Texas)

*A word that reads the same backward or forward.

Cashtown, Pennsylvania. *Cashtown* was named in the early 1830s after a store owner declared only cash could be used for all goods and services.

Climax, Minnesota. This small town in northern Minnesota was named in the 1890s after a member of the well-to-do Seenerson family found some Climax Chewing Tobacco on the ground while moving into their new home. Since the settlement was nameless, a decision was made to call it *Climax.*

Coarsegold, California. When a nineteenth-century miner found gold in nuggets rather than in dust, he commemorated his find by naming the area *Coarsegold.*

Death Valley, California. *Death Valley* was named in 1849 when a band of gold seekers got lost in this desolate desert known for its excessive heat and blistering sun. Although they named it *Death Valley,* only one of the miners in the group lost his life.

Detour, Maryland. This small town, formerly named Double Pipe Creek, was renamed in 1905 after the Western Railroad laid tracks through the area and insisted that the

---

Travel America in Illinois or Arkansas

The next time you go on vacation and want to visit a lot of places but have a limited time and budget, head straight to Illinois or Arkansas. In Illinois you will find towns named *Kansas, Ohio, Oregon, Tennessee, Vermont, Virginia,* and *Wyoming.* The state of Arkansas hosts towns by the name of *Augusta, Bismarck, Charleston, Cleveland, Columbus, Concord, Danville, Denver, Evansville, Helena, Houston, Monticello, Nashville, Omaha, Tupelo,* and *Waterloo.*

---

town use a shorter name to fit on its forms. A town meeting was held to name the town when Daniel P. Saylor, who had done some traveling in the Midwest, suggested the word *Detour*, simply because he liked it. Although some people feel neither Saylor nor his neighbors knew what the word meant, the town kept the name.

See the World in Maine

If your budget doesn't permit you to travel abroad, but you want to boast to your friends how worldly you are, head for the state of Maine. There you will find towns by the name of *Athens, Belfast, Belgrade, Bremen, China, Denmark, Dresden, Frankfurt, Limerick, Lisbon, Madrid, Mexico, Naples, Norway, Oxford, Palermo, Paris, Peru, Poland, Rome,* and *Vienna.* Just think of the impressive postcards you can send back home!

Dime Box, Texas. A neighborly practice at rural post offices once involved placing a box on the front porch into which people could deposit money for underpaid or postage-due letters. That's how *Dime Box* got its name.

Embarrass, Wisconsin. This small town in northeastern Wisconsin was named by French Canadian loggers. They called the river on which the town sits *Riviere Embarrass*, which means "to obstruct," "to entangle," or "to impede" in French. The river was shallow and rocky, and consequently, logs that were floated from upstream were constantly getting stuck. It was later renamed the Embarrass River (giving it an English-sounding name) and when the town was incorporated in 1895, it too was called *Embarrass*.

Evening Shade, Arkansas. This small town is the namesake of "Evening Shade," a television show starring Burt Reynolds. Although the town does not appear in the show, tourists flock to see it and buy souvenirs. It is said that Hillary Rodham Clinton suggested the name for the show.

Gas, Kansas. *Gas* was named in 1893 when drillers in search of natural gas struck it big. In the next few decades numerous companies moved in to exploit the resources, and the town became one of the biggest suppliers in the nation. Although the town ran out of gas in 1910, the name still lives on.

Harmony, California. This small town started as the site of a creamery in the 1860s. Feuding dairy farmers got out of hand and a farmer was shot. Following the tragedy, the town's farmers promised to live in harmony with each other, and thus the town was named.

Hungry Horse, Montana. This town was named after Montana's severe winter of 1901–1902. Legend has it that some horses were lost and later found, alive and hungry, during this brutal winter.

Jackpot, Nevada. This small gambling town was named in the 1950s by its townspeople because of all the coins their slot machines spit out.

Jenny Jump, New Jersey. Supposedly, this town was named after a local girl named Jenny jumped off a cliff while running away from attacking Indians.

Jot 'Em Down, Texas. *Jot 'Em Down* was named in the early 1930s by its townspeople, who were avid fans of "Lum and Abner," one of the nation's favorite radio shows. They named their town after the show's commissary the Jot 'Em Down general store.

King and Queen Court House, Virginia. This town was named in the 1690s after King William and Queen Mary, the British monarchs who acquired Virginia as one of their colonies in the New World. The settlers called their village King and Queen County in honor of them. The name soon changed to *King and Queen Court House,* since it was customary to call the county seat—the place where the courthouse is located—by the county name followed by *Court House.*

Some Places Aren't Where You'd Expect Them to Be

If you're looking for Virginia City, don't go to Virginia but to Nevada. And Michigan City isn't in Michigan but in Pennsylvania. And the Mississippi River neither starts nor ends in Mississippi. It starts in Minnesota and ends in Louisiana. And if anyone asks you which is farther west, Virginia or West Virginia, the answer is Virginia.

Towns That Border Two or More States

Some places border two states, and one, Kenova, West Virginia, borders three. So what do you call such a town? Read on and you'll find out.

Arkoma, Okla. (Arkansas, Oklahoma)
Calexico, Calif. (a state and nation: California and Mexico)
Delmar, Del. (Delaware, Maryland)
Kanorado, Kans. (Kansas, Colorado)
Kenova, W. Va. (Kentucky, Ohio, West Virginia)
Mardela Springs, Md. (Maryland, Delaware)
Moark, Ark. (Missouri, Arkansas)
Tennga, Ga. (Tennessee, Georgia)
Texarkana, Ark. (Texas, Arkansas)
Texhoma, Okla., Tex. (Texas, Oklahoma)
Texico, N. Mex. (Texas, New Mexico)
Vershire, Vt. (Vermont, New Hampshire)

Musical Town Names

Professor Harold Hill, the leading character of Meredith Willson's *The Music Man*, would have loved these musical towns. And perhaps maybe their founders would have been more receptive to a marching band than were those in River City, Iowa!

Alto (towns in five states)	Fluteville, Conn.
Bass, Ark.	Horner, W. Va.
Bow, Ky., Wash.	Organ, N. Mex.
Drum, Ky.	Singer, La.
Drums, Pa.	Solo, Mo.
Fiddletown, Calif.	Triangle (towns in three states)
Fife (towns in three states)	Trio, S.C.

Leap, Oregon. This town was named in a leap year.

Likely, California. At a town meeting called to name the township, someone stood up and announced, "It isn't likely that we will agree on any name." The townspeople, in fact, agreed upon the name *Likely*.

Midnight, Mississippi. This small farming town was named following a poker game in the late 1800s. One lucky farmer won the land during a high-stakes contest and exclaimed, "Well, boys. It's midnight, and that's exactly what I'm going to call the land I just won. Let's quit." And the name has stuck ever since.

Moscow, Texas. When the townspeople applied for the name Grenville, there were more than a dozen towns by that name in the United States. When the post office suggested they pick a name of a city that was as far away as they could imagine, they picked Moscow, Russia.

Mount Healthy, Ohio. *Mount Healthy* was named by the grateful survivors of a cholera epidemic in the 1850s.

Ninety-six, South Carolina. This town is 96 miles from Cherokee, South Carolina, which was the nearest trading center when the town was named.

Notrees, Texas. This town was named *Notrees* because it was so barren, which tells it all for this otherwise nondescript town.

Naughty Girl Meadow, Oregon. This town was called *Whorehouse Meadow*, which accurately described activity there before its name was changed to *Naughty Girl Meadow* in 1890. The meadow is on a mountain route once used by shepherds to move their flocks to pasture and market. Evidently, some resourceful prostitutes pitched camp and lured the passing sheep men into what were literally tents of ill repute. (Interestingly, the meadow is near Honeymoon Lake.)

Old Glory, Texas. *Old Glory* was named in 1917 by the townspeople to show their patriotic support for the United States in World War I.

Parachute, Colorado. *Parachute* was named during the late 1800s after a surveyor compared the land's crazy contour to that of the tight lines of a falling parachute.

Parade, South Dakota. *Parade* was named in 1920 to honor the man who donated the land. Although the man's last name was *Paradee,* the last *e* in the name was accidentally cut off when the name was filed.

97

Paradox, Colorado. *Paradox* was named after the valley in which it sits in western Colorado. The surveyors for the area named this valley in 1876 because it measured 23 miles in length and five miles in width. The paradox is that the Dolores River, which bisects the valley, cuts across the width instead of running down the length like most other streams and rivers.

Peculiar, Missouri. This town was named out of frustration after the townspeople had unsuccessfully tried to name it Lincoln, Jefferson, Washington, and several other names that were rejected by the post office because cities with those names already existed in the state. Exasperated, the town leaders wrote to the post office authorities and said: "Call us any peculiar name you want, just send our mail!"

Company Towns

The following towns were named after their major business or industry.

Alcoa, Tenn. (Aluminum Company of America)
Atlo, N.J. (Atlantic Transport Co.)
Charmco, W.Va. (Charleston Milling Co.)
El Segundo, Calif. (for a company's second refinery)
Excello, Ohio (Excello Paper Co.)
Guardian, W. Va. (Guardian Coal and Oil Co.)
Hatboro, Pa. (home of an eighteenth-century hatter)
Katy, Tex. (Missouri, Kansas, and Texas Railroad—"Katy")
Latexo, Tex. (Louisiana-Texas Orchards)
Lobeco, S.C. (Long, Bellamy and Co.)
Paramount, Calif. (movie studios)
Tolu, Ky. (local whiskey-based tonic)

An Irishman's Delight

According to the U.S. Postal Service, there are more than 160 cities and towns in the United States with *Green* in their name. There are Greenvilles and Greenwoods, Green Bays and Green Islands, and just plain Greens—oodles of them. There are even a couple of Shamrocks, in Texas and Oklahoma, and Missouri has a Saint Patrick.

Pointblank, Texas. A sharpshooting woman in this area, who was nearly as good as Annie Oakley, remarked that where she lived, the view was so clear that one might shoot point-blank in any direction.

Reform, Alabama. *Reform* was named by Methodist missionary Lorenzo Dow in 1819. After unsuccessfully trying to calm down the town's rowdy citizens, the evangelist packed up his belongings and headed out. One of the rowdy locals shouted after him, "We don't have a name for our town. Got a suggestion?" "Reform!" shouted the disappointed missionary.

Rifle, Colorado. *Rifle* was named by a land surveyor who, with his assistant, was sketching the land deep in the Grand Hog Back Range. They realized that they forgot their rifle which was their only means of protection against wild animals and the fierce Indians of the area. The surveyor sent his assistant with a rough sketch of the spot where he remembered leaving his rifle propped against a tree by a creek. Because of this map, he chose the name *Rifle*.

Rolla, Missouri. This town was named by accident. The townspeople originally wanted to name it Raleigh after the birthplace of one of its citizens, but the application to the post office department spelled the name *Rolla*, just as the Southerner pronounced it.

Rough and Ready, California. This town was named during the Gold Rush in 1849 by Captain A. A. Townsend, who served under General "Rough and Ready" Zachary Taylor. Townsend came to the area from Wisconsin with a gold-mining crew he called the Rough and Ready. The town was named after this crew.

Skull Valley, Arizona. *Skull Valley* was named by the first white settlers of the area who arrived in 1864. They found piles of Indian skulls, which were remnants of a battle that had been fought between Apache and Maracopa warriors.

Slapout, Oklahoma. This tiny town located at the east end of the Oklahoma panhandle was renamed in the 1930s by construction workers who were installing a highway for the Works Progress Administration. They would often go to a store in Nye, a nearby town, to get supplies. When they came back empty-handed, they would say the store was "slapout" of supplies. Thus, the area became known as *Slapout* instead of Nye.

Sleepy Eye, Minnesota. *Sleepy Eye* was named in the late 1800s for Sioux Chief Sleepy Eye, who had been a very popular peacemaker in Minnesota.

Smut Eye, Alabama. This small town in southeastern Alabama was named for the bad habits of its men in the early nineteenth century. The big hangout of the area was the blacksmith's shop, where the men would play games, trade stories, and drink moonshine. The men would come home with blackened eyes. Their popular excuse to their wives was that it was from the smut from the blacksmith's shop, hence the name *Smut Eye*.

Lake What's Its Name

Long before Europeans settled in the area, the Nipmuck Indians gathered at the large lake (on its shores is now the town of Webster, Massachusetts—population 15,201). The Nipmuck called this lake *Chargoggagoggmanchauggagoggcaubunagunga-maugg.* Loosely translated, the name means: "knifemen or Englishmen at Manchaug at fishing place of the boundary." Another interpretation of the long name is: "you fish on your side, I fish on my side, nobody fishes in the middle." In 1935, the Massachusetts Legislature officially named it Lake Chargoggagoggmanchauggagoggcaubunagungamaugg. It is the longest name of any place in the United States and is said to rank third in the world after places in Australia and Wales.

Stillwater, Ohio. The local Indians were told that if they would give up their claim to some land, a nearby stream would be made to flow with alcohol. Later, the Indians said that they had been lied to and the stream was "still water."

Sweet Lips, Tennessee. Legend has it that this small town was named during the mid-nineteenth century after a passing traveler commented on the water in the stream. "Oh, that's so sweet to my lips!" the exhausted traveler exclaimed.

Telephone, Texas. This small town in northeastern Texas was named during the late 1870s to honor Alexander Graham Bell's new invention, the telephone. It just happened to be perfect timing that the town was in search of a new name when the announcement of the miraculous new invention was made.

Tenino, Washington. This town was named *Tenino*, pronounced "ten-nine-oh," because it sits 1,090 feet above sea level.

Ten Sleep, Wyoming. There are many different stories about how this small town got its name. *Ten Sleep* was located between two well-known Indian camps during the mid-1800s. Indians measured distance by the number of nights, or "sleeps," it took to travel a certain distance. Thus, some say the town was named because it took ten sleeps to get from either of those camps to *Ten Sleep*. Others think the town was named because a tribe waited at this location for "ten sleeps" while waiting for others to join them. Still others say they stayed there because they were snowed in or because there was a battle with another tribe that lasted "ten sleeps."

Tightwad, Missouri. According to legend, *Tightwad* received its name years ago when a postman stopped at the local store to pay for a watermelon that he would pick up after he had finished his route. At the end of the day, he returned for his watermelon and found that the merchant had sold it to another customer for a higher price. The postman called the store owner a tightwad, and the name *Tightwad* was kept when the town was incorporated in 1894.

Tin Cup, Colorado. This small town in the Rockies was named during the 1860s by Jim Taylor, a Southerner looking for gold, which he found while panning in a creek about five miles west of the Continental Divide. He kept the gold in a tin drinking cup and named the area Tin Cup Gulch, which eventually became a mining town called *Tin Cup*.

Toad Hop, Indiana. Whenever the creek that ran through this small town overflowed in the spring, toads would swarm the area. Thus it was named *Toad Hop*.

Descriptive U.S. Place-names

Sometimes things get named because of the way they look. The following U.S. places were named for their obvious appearances:

AB Mountains, Arkansas—when the snow melts the letters *A* and *B* appear, due to rock formations.

Angleworm Lake, Michigan—a long, narrow, and crooked lake.

Belt Mountains, Montana—a beltlike layer of white rock bisects a butte.

Book Cliffs, Utah—resembles a set of books on a shelf.

Bosom, Wyoming—these two peaks look like a bosom.

Camelback Mountain, Arizona—this mountain looks like the hump on a camel's back.

Chetlo, Oregon—the Chinook word for "oyster," describes the shape of this lake.

Chickenbone Lake, Michigan—this lake is shaped like a wishbone.

Chinese Wall, Wyoming—a long, wall-like formation.

Cowhorn Mountain, Oregon—this mountain has two pinnacles shaped like a cow's horns.

Mount Derby, Colorado—this mountain is shaped like a hat.

Fluted Rock, Arizona—these rocks look like organ pipes.

Mitten Butte, Arizona—this mountain looks like a pair of mittens.

Moose Lake, California—this lake is shaped like the head of a moose.

Music Mountain, Arizona—the rock strata look like a musical staff.

Preacher's Head, New Mexico—it looks like the head of a serious man.

Saw Buck Mountain, Arizona—this mountain is shaped like the *X* of a sawhorse.

Valley of Fire, Nevada—these rocks are bright red.

Trebloc, Mississippi. When the town's postmaster, whose name was Colbert, submitted the name *Colbert* to the U.S. Post Office, it was rejected. He then deliberately reversed the spelling of his name and submitted the name *Trebloc,* which was accepted.

Tropic, Utah. *Tropic* was named because its climate is tropical compared to nearby communities. The terrain surrounding the town keeps the good weather in and the bad weather out.

Truth or Consequences, New Mexico. This town was originally called Hot Springs until a popular radio game show called "Truth or Consequences" advertised that if some town in the United States would rename itself after the show, the program would be broadcast from there each year. Hot Springs accepted the radio show's proposition and changed its name.

Turkey Scratch, Arkansas. This small town was named for the abundant wild turkeys in the area. While the spot had been an excellent hunting ground for a large variety of game, it was only after early settlers brought in wild turkeys that the area became a haven for the big birds. Hunters noticed how the turkeys scratched fallen leaves when they searched for food, and they referred to the area as *Turkey Scratch.*

Two Dot, Montana. This town was named after the man who donated the land for the townsite. Cattleman "Two Dot" Wilson, who branded his cattle with two dots, gets credit for this name.

Two Eggs, Florida. This town was originally called Allison until the early 1920s. Henry and Attaway Barnes would trek four miles to the nearest general store to get groceries for a neighbor. They would buy fourteen eggs—12 for the neighbor and two as their pay. The store owner referred to them as the "two-egg boys," and before long the settlement became known as *Two Eggs*.

Uncertain, Texas. *Uncertain* was accidentally named when the town was incorporated. Since the townspeople couldn't agree on a name when they filled out the incorporation papers, they wrote "uncertain," thinking they would eventually come up with something more appropriate. As funny as it sounds, the state thought this is what they wanted to name the town.

Virgin, Utah. This small town in southwestern Utah was named by its early settlers. They were so impressed with the clarity of the water, they settled on its banks and called the river *Virgin*, the name that was later given to their community.

Waterproof, Louisiana. This town was named *Waterproof* after it was relocated to higher ground due to frequent flooding.

Why Do We Call Greenland *Green?*

Greenland, the largest island in the world, is mostly covered by ice and snow, and should therefore have appropriately been named *Whiteland*. It is believed that in A.D. 985 Eric the Red named it Greenland to induce colonists from Iceland to inhabit the new island. Others believe that Eric the Red was not actually conning his followers, but was unaware of its ice-covered interior plateau, since he may have only visited Greenland's ice-free western coast in midsummer.

■

How Nations Around the World Were Named

Here's an interesting list of nations and what their names mean:

Algeria: Arabic "the islands"
Argentina: Latin "silvery"
Australia: Latin *terra australis,* "southern land"
Austria: Latin "eastern land"
Belgium: Gallic "brave, warlike"
Bolivia: Simon Bolivar, "The Liberator"
Brazil: Portuguese *terra de brasil* "land of brazilwood"
Canada: Iroquoin "cabin"
Chile: Araucanian "cold, winter"
China: from the Ch'in dynasty
Colombia: after Christopher Columbus
Denmark: Germanic "territory of the Dane tribe"
Dominican Republic: Spanish "the Lord's day" (Sunday)
Ecuador: Spanish "equator"
El Salvador: Spanish "the savior"
England: Old English *Englaland,* "land of the Angles"
Ethiopia: Greek "people with sunburnt faces"
Finland: Swedish "land of the Finn tribe"
France: Germanic "Franks, freemen"
Germany: Latin form of tribal name possibly meaning "strong hands"
Greece: possibly "venerable people"
Haiti: native word for "mountains"
Honduras: Spanish "depths"
Hungary: "tribe who lived by River Ugra"
Iceland: "land of ice"
India: from Indus River
Indonesia: Indian and Greek word for "island"
Iran: Sanskrit "worthy"
Iraq: Arabic "shore, lowland"
Ireland: Erse "western" or "green"

Israel: Hebrew "god isra"
Italy: "land of Vitali tribe"
Jamaica: Arawak "island of springs"
Japan: Chinese "land of rising sun"
Jordan: from Jordan River
Kuwait: Arabic "the enclosed" or "little port"
Lebanon: Hebrew "white mountain"
Liberia: Latin "free"
Mexico: Nahuatl *Mexitli*, war god
Monaco: Greek "monk"
Netherlands: "low-lying lands"
New Zealand: "new Zeeland" (Dutch province)
Niger/Nigeria: from River Niger, "flowing water"
Paraguay: from river name meaning "water"
Philippines: for Philip II of Spain
Poland: Slavonic "plain dwellers"
Portugal: Latin "warm harbor"
Romania: "people from Rome"
Saudi Arabia: from the king Ibn-Saud
Scotland: "Scots' land", the Scots possibly being "wanderers"
Singapore: Sanskrit "lion town"
Spain: Latin *Hispania*, their name for the Iberian peninsula
Sudan: Arabic "country of the black people"
Sweden: Swedish "Svea kingdom"
Switzerland: from the canton name Schwyz
Tanzania: Tanganyika and Zanzibar, which were united in 1964.
Thailand: native words "country of the free"
Venezuela: Spanish "little Venice"
Vietnam: Annamese "land of the south"
Wales: Briton "foreigners"
Yugoslavia: Slavonic "southern slaves"
Zambia: from Zambezi River

Wewanta, West Virginia. The locals of this small town decided they needed a post office. They wrote to the Post Office Department in Washington, D.C., saying: "Wewanta post office." They got their post office.

Zzyzx, California. This small town was originally called Soda Springs due to its large salt deposits. In 1944 entrepreneurs Curtis and Helen Springer built a huge health resort there and renamed the town *Zzyzx* (pronounced "Zye-zix") because they wanted to have a name at the end of the alphabet to assure them of having the "last word."

Presidential Nicknames

■

National public figures in America are public domain and therefore fair game. In particular, the news media love to give them nicknames. For example, every U.S. president has had at least one handle whether favorable or unfavorable, colorful or dull. The following is a chronological list of presidential nicknames and the stories behind them.

George Washington. George Washington had three popular nicknames. He was called the *Deliverer of America* for his service during the revolutionary war as commander-in-chief of the Continental army. Washington was also known as the *Father of His Country* because he took such an active role in shaping America into an independent nation. Others called him the *Surveyor President* because he was a surveyor during his youth.

John Adams. Adams is known as the *Father of American Independence* because he was responsible for securing the adoption of the Declaration of Independence. He was also called the *Duke of Braintree* because his birthplace was Braintree, Mass., where he retired after his political career.

Thomas Jefferson. Thomas Jefferson is nicknamed the *Father of the Declaration of Independence* because he drafted and wrote the original document.

James Monroe. The period during Monroe's administration from 1817–1825 was known as the Era of Good Feeling. Thus Monroe is most popularly known as the *Era-of-Good-Feeling President.*

John Quincy Adams. John Quincy Adams has two nicknames. He was called the *Accidental President* because he won 13 out of 24 electoral votes in the election of 1824. His contemporaries said that one of the votes had been cast by mistake and thus "it was an accident that he got a majority of the votes." Adams was also called the *Old Man Eloquent* because of his great public speaking and his ability to masterfully debate his side of an issue.

Andrew Jackson. Andrew Jackson is called the *General* because he served as major-general in the United States Army. Jackson was named *Old Hickory* by his soldiers because he disobeyed orders from Secretary of War John Armstrong, in order to stay loyal to his soldiers and help the ill and wounded. They said he was "tough as hickory" in reference to his defiance of the secretary's orders.

Martin Van Buren. Martin Van Buren was often called the *Fox* and the *Little Magician* because he was such a clever and wily politician. He was also called *King Martin the First* because he was such a close friend and personal advisor of Andrew Jackson, who was known as "King Andrew the First."

William H. Harrison. William Harrison was called the *Hero of Tippecanoe* because he was the leader at the Battle of Tippecanoe in 1811. The *Farmer President* was attached to him as a result of his farming background and his interest in protecting the rights of farmers.

John Tyler. Tyler is known as the *Accidental President* because he took over as president when William Henry Harrison died on April 4, 1841.

James Polk. James Polk was often called the *First Dark Horse* because he was unexpectedly elected. Martin Van Buren had been eliminated as a candidate at the Democratic Convention of 1844, and Polk became the party's presidential candidate. He was also commonly called *Young Hickory* because like Andrew Jackson ("Old Hickory") he was raised amid the hardships of frontier life, and he shared Jackson's political views and policies.

Zachary Taylor. Zachary Taylor was named *Old Rough and Ready* by the soldiers under his command during the Mexican War while stationed in Monterrey, Mexico, in 1847 because he was a tough disciplinarian with his troops. He also always wore plain, serviceable clothing as a result of his dislike of any unnecessary display of military ceremony. Taylor was also called *Old Zach* by his friends and associates.

Millard Fillmore. Fillmore was also known as the *Accidental President* because he automatically became president when Zachary Taylor died on July 9, 1850.

Franklin Pierce. Franklin Pierce was often referred to as *Handsome Frank* because of his good looks.

James Buchanan. Buchanan was called the *Bachelor President* because he never married (becoming the only single U.S. president). His friends called him *Old Buck,* short for Buchanan.

Abraham Lincoln. Lincoln was nicknamed the *Emancipation President* because slavery was abolished during his administration. He is also known as *Honest Abe,* attributed to his reputation for having a high standard of honesty and integrity.

Andrew Johnson. Andrew Johnson's most popular nickname was *His Accidency* because he took over as president when Abraham Lincoln was assassinated. He was also called *Sir Veto* and the *Veto President* by his political enemies because he vetoed 22 bills passed by Congress.

Ulysses S. Grant. Ulysses S. Grant was called the *American Caesar* because his political enemies feared he might be elected to a third term and become tyrannical. He was called *Butcher Grant* because so many of his soldiers were killed trying to conquer the Confederates.

Rutherford B. Hayes. Democrats called Hayes the *Dark Horse President, the Fraud President,* and the *President de facto* because he won the presidency in 1876 against Democratic candidate Samuel Jones Tilden within such a narrow margin and on such shaky grounds. Tilden received 184 electoral votes while Hayes received 163. A controversy arose over 22 Southern electoral votes so Congress decided to settle the dispute by appointing an electoral commission composed of five senators, five representatives, and five members of the Supreme Court. Their decision, based on a vote of eight to seven, ended up giving the 22 electoral votes to Hayes; thus he was elected president having a total of 185 electoral votes to Tilden's 184.

James Garfield. Garfield was called the *Canal Boy* because he was a steersman of a boat on the Ohio Canal during his teens. He was called the *Martyr President* after his death because he was assassinated about six months and two weeks after his inauguration.

Chester Arthur. Arthur was often called the *First Gentleman of the Land* and *Prince Arthur* because he was such a well-dressed, handsome, charming man. He was also known as *Chet* by his friends and associates as an abbreviation of Chester. Along with other presidents who took office after their predecessor's death, Arthur is known as *His Accidency* because he became president after James Garfield died.

Grover Cleveland. Cleveland was called the *Buffalo Sheriff* because he was the sheriff of Erie County, N.Y., with his main office in Buffalo. Others called him the *People's President* because he consistently advocated policies that served the interests of the people.

Benjamin Harrison. Harrison was most commonly called *Little Ben* in allusion to his physical appearance. He had a large stocky body set on small, short legs.

William McKinley. McKinley was nicknamed the *Idol of Ohio* because he was such a good-hearted, kind, democratic native of Ohio. People also called him *Prosperity's Advance Agent* because the economy prospered greatly during his administration.

Theodore Roosevelt. Theodore Roosevelt's most popular nickname was *Bull Moose* because he told reporters he "felt like a bull moose" after accepting his nomination for candidate of the Progressive Party. But mostly, he was simply called *Teddy*.

William Howard Taft. Taft was most commonly known as *Big Bill* because he was such a large and influential man.

113

Woodrow Wilson. Wilson was often called the *Phrase Maker* because he coined so many phrases to inspire patriotism during the First World War. He was also called the *School Master in Politics* because before he entered the world of politics, he had taught in many of the nation's finest colleges and universities. Wilson had a Ph.D. in political science and was a noted historian. Prior to entering politics, he taught at Princeton University.

Calvin Coolidge. Calvin Coolidge's boyhood friends called him *Red* because his hair was bright red. He was also known as *Silent Cal* because he preferred to keep his plans and politics to himself, having a philosophy that those things left unsaid would never harm him.

Herbert Hoover. Herbert Hoover is known as the *Chief* because of the great influence he exerted as secretary of commerce from 1917 until 1921. The *Man of Great Heart* stems from the large number of philanthropic projects he initiated.

Franklin D. Roosevelt. Franklin D. Roosevelt was most commonly referred to by his initials, *FDR*, which the press liked to use because it looked good in the headlines. Others called him the *Boss* because Congress granted him emergency powers to deal with the nation's economic crisis. He was also called the *Squire of Hyde Park* because his family home was in Hyde Park on the Hudson in New York.

Harry S Truman. Truman's most popular nickname was *Give 'em Hell Harry* because he gave the Republican party such a hard time with his sharp comments. Truman, a Democrat, once joked about "Republican firemen . . . too busy playing a game of political checkers to go put the fire out."

Dwight David Eisenhower. Eisenhower's most popular nickname is *Ike*. His classmates gave him the nickname *Little Ike* to distinguish him from "Big Ike," his older brother Edgar.

John Fitzgerald Kennedy. Kennedy was most frequently referred to by his initials, *JFK*.

Lyndon B. Johnson. Johnson's most popular nickname was *Landslide Lyndon* because he won the 1964 election in such a landslide. He was also referred to by his initials, *LBJ*.

Richard M. Nixon. Nixon's most popular nickname was *Tricky Dick* because he was such a wily politician. After Watergate, *Tricky Dick* was a name that history would never forget. Interestingly, as a kid, his favorite book was *Tom Sawyer* because of Tom's intelligent tricks.

Gerald Ford. Ford was most popularly known simply as *Gerry*, a nickname for Gerald. Ford was such a down-to-earth man that the name fit him well.

Jimmy Carter. Although he was most frequently called *Jimmy*, the *Peanut President* was a nickname applied to him because he operated a peanut farm in Georgia before his life in politics.

Ronald Reagan. Reagan's most popular nickname is *Dutch*, given to him by his father Jack Reagan after he was born. His father bragged about his "fat little Dutchman" because he weighed 10 pounds at birth. He was also called the *Teflon President* because while criticism was levied at him, no scandal or trouble stuck.

George Bush. One of Bush's most popular nicknames is *George "No New Taxes" Bush* because of his ill-fated promises not to levy any new taxes. Other Bush nicknames include

115

Poppy, which came from his grandfather's nickname "Pop," and *Skip*, a preppy name he picked up when attending Yale University and often referred to in Garry Trudeau's comic strip "Doonesbury."

Bill Clinton. During his presidential campaign, Bill Clinton was called *Slick Willie* by those who opposed him. This unflattering nickname was an effort to make him appear as a slippery character. A fan of Elvis Presley and a rather charismatic figure himself, Clinton was also dubbed "Elvis" by the press.

Politics in the Family

Three U.S. presidents had the same family name as their related predecessors. John Quincy Adams was the son of John Adams; Benjamin Harrison was the grandson of William Henry Harrison; and Franklin Delano Roosevelt was a fifth cousin of Theodore Roosevelt.

Presidential Name Changes

Six U.S. presidents began life with different names. Ulysses Simpson Grant was originally Hiram Ulysses Grant; Grover Cleveland began as Stephen Grover Cleveland; Woodrow Wilson was originally Thomas Woodrow Wilson; Calvin Coolidge was John Calvin Coolidge; Dwight David Eisenhower was David Dwight Eisenhower; and Gerald Ford took the name of his adopted father but was originally named after his biological father, Leslie Lynch King.

Native American Tribal Names

■

Have you ever wondered how certain Native American tribes were named? Tribe names have interesting meanings in their native tongues—with the exception of those names that were given by a rival tribe (in which case they were not always friendly or flattering.)

Apache. The Apache Indians were a fierce tribe that inhabited Arizona and New Mexico. The word *apache* means "enemy" and is derived from the Indian word, "apachu," a word from the Zuni tribe.

Arapaho. The name of this native tribe of Wyoming and Oklahoma means "mother of tribes."

Assiniboine. This tribe lived in the Lake Superior region of what is now Minnesota. The word "Assiniboine" means "those who cook with stones."

Blackfoot. The name of this tribe is a Cree term meaning "blackfoot people," in reference to black-dyed moccasins. The Blackfoot lived mostly in Montana and Alberta.

Caddo. The name of this tribe from the area that is now Arkansas and Oklahoma means "real chiefs."

Catawba. This tribe made their original home in the territory that is now the border region between the Carolinas. These village dwellers depended heavily upon agriculture for food and located their villages in river valleys. The word *Catawba* means "people of the river."

Cherokee. The name of this large tribe means "people of a different speech," a name given to the tribe by the neighboring Creeks.

Cheyenne. The name of this tribe of Colorado, Montana, and Wyoming means "red talkers," a name given to them by the Sioux.

Chippewa (Ojibwa). The Chippewas were one of the largest and most powerful tribes and inhabited the country of the west Great Lakes. The Chippewas spoke Algonquian, and their name is a reference to a puckered seam in the style of the tribe's moccasins. The Chippewas also called themselves *Anishinabe*, which means "first men."

Chiricahua. This Apache tribe located in southwestern Arizona has a name meaning "great mountains."

Choctaw. With the exception of the Cherokee, the Choctaws were the largest single tribe in the southeast. It is said that the Choctaw and the Chickasaw tribes were once joined together by two brothers, Chahtah and Chikasah. At some point in time, the two groups split, taking the names of each of the two brothers.

Comanche. The actual meaning of the name *Comanche* is not known, but it is believed to be a Spanish adaptation of an Indian word. These proud and powerful people, known for their rugged individualism and fierceness in battle, have been referred to as "lords of the southern plains."

Conestoga. The name of the Conestoga people of Pennsylvania means "beautiful magic land."

Cree. This large Canadian Algonquian tribe occupied a large area south of Hudson Bay in the early seventeenth century and later migrated west to the Plains in the eighteenth century. *Cree* is a short form of *Kristenaux*, a French corruption of one of their own names for themselves.

Crow. The members of this tribe, which formerly lived along the Missouri River and later settled in the Rocky Mountains, called themselves *Apsaaloke*, or "crow people." They were called *gens de corbeaux* by the French explorers, which means "people of the ravens," and eventually *Crow* in English.

Flathead. This tribe in Montana is known as "Flatheads" and also as the Salish Indians. Actually the name should be attributed to another Salishan-speaking tribe along the Northwest Coast that practiced a custom known as "head-flattening." It involved a gradual process of deforming the head by tying a padded board to the forehead. The French fur trappers started calling the interior Salish by this name—it was a case of mistaken identity—and for this reason, the Salish Indians in Montana were called Flatheads.

Hopi. The Hopi were once a large and powerful tribe in northeast Arizona. Their name in the Hopitu language means "the peaceful ones" or "all peaceful."

Huma. The name of this Choctaw tribe in what is now Louisiana means "red people."

Kickapoo. This midwestern tribe lived in territories that are today Kansas, Oklahoma, Wisconsin, and Mexico. They

119

called themselves *Kiwegapawz*, which means "he who moves about, stand now here, now there."

Menominee. The name of this Indiana tribe derives from the word *Manoomini* in the Ojibwa language, and means "wild rice eaters."

Miami. This tribe lived on the southern shores of Lake Michigan. Their name is an Ojibwa word that means "people of the peninsula."

Mohave (or **Mojave**). The name of this tribe, which lives along the Colorado River in Arizona, means "beside the water."

Mohawk. The name of the Mohawk tribe, which originally lived in New York State, is derived from the Narragansett word *mohowawog*, or "man eaters." They were probably given this name by their enemies.

Natchez. The name of this tribe, which dwelled in the area that is now lower Mississippi, means "warriors of the high bluff."

Osage. The designation of this tribe, which lived originally in the Ohio River Valley, is a name they called themselves meaning "children of the middle waters."

Ottawa. The name of this tribe native to Michigan and southeastern Canada means "traders." It is derived from the French word *Outaouois*, after the Ojibwa word *Odaawaa*.

Paiute. The name of the Paiute is derived from the Shoshonean *pah-ute* and means "true water."

Papago. This tribe's name means "bean people," and was given them by the neighboring Pimas. The tribe lived in the Sonoran Desert near what is now the border of southwest Arizona and northwest Sonora, a state of Mexico.

Passamaquoddy. The name of this tribe, native to Maine and New Brunswick, comes from the Micmac word *pestemo-kati*, meaning "many fish."

Pawnee. This tribe, which dwelled on the Great Plains, has a name that comes from the Caddoan word *pariki*, which means "horn," in reference to the upright and curved scalplock hairstyle that the tribe members wore. It is also possible that the name might be derived from the word *parisu*, which means "hunter."

Penobscot. This Maine tribe's name means "the rocky place," a reference to the rocky falls in the river of the same name, where the tribe has long resided.

Pensacola. The name of this tribe (and the city in Florida) comes from the Choctaw *paši okla* or "hairy people."

Peoria. The name of this tribe (and the town in Illinois) comes from the Illinois *peouareoua* meaning "place of fat beasts."

Ponca. The name of this tribe in the Dakotas and Oklahoma means "scarred head."

Potawatomi. This tribe, which inhabited the land between Lake Huron and Lake Michigan, has an Algonquian name that means "people of the place of fire."

Pueblo. This group of tribes (ancestors to the Zuni and the Hopi) lived in the New Mexico and Arizona areas, the word *pueblo* refers to the permanent stone or adobe villages in which these people lived.

Quapaw. The name of this Arkansas tribe means "downstream people." These migrant people were the southwestern branch of the Sioux, who followed the Mississippi and Arkansas rivers.

Seminole. The name of this tribe in Florida means "one who has camped out from the regular towns" or "runaway." The name results from Seminole ancestors who broke off from other tribes living in Georgia and Alabama during the 1700s.

Seneca. The name of this tribe which dwelled in western New York, means "great hill people." To other members of the Iroquois league, the Seneca tribe is known as "keepers of the western door," or the "door-keepers."

Shawnee. The Shawnees dwelled in an area that is now Tennessee, Kentucky, Ohio, and West Virginia. Their name in the Algonquian language means "southerners."

Shoshone. This Wyoming tribe's name means "sheep-eaters."

Sioux. Also known as the Dakota tribe, they lived in South Dakota, North Dakota, Montana, Nebraska, and Minnesota. The name of this large tribe is derived from an Ojibwa term, *Nadowe-is-iw*, meaning "adder," thus "enemy." The word "Sioux" is a French version of the Ojibwa word. The Sioux called themselves *Oceti Sakowin* or "Seven Council Fires," in reference to their seven political divisions: Mdewakanton, Sisseton, Wahpeton, Wahpekute, Yankton, Yanktonai, and Teton.

Taos. This tribe from New Mexico has a name from the Tiwa language meaning "red willow place," in reference to their pueblo called Ilaphai.

Tuskegee. The name of this tribe (and the city in Alabama) means "warriors."

Ute. This tribe resided in what is now Utah and Colorado, and its name means "high up" or "land of the sun."

Wallawalla. The Wallawallas lived in northern Oregon and southern Washington. Their name means "little river."

Wichita. The tribe occupied what is now Kansas, Oklahoma, and Texas and was named by the French, who called the members "Picts" from the French word *pique*. This was a result of the tattoos on their faces and bodies that were pricked onto their skins to make elaborate designs.

Winnebago. The name of this tribe, which dwelled originally in what is now Wisconsin, is derived from the Fox word meaning "dirty water" or "people of the stinking water place."

Wyandot. The name of this tribe, which lived originally in Ontario, Michigan, and Ohio, means "islanders."

Yakima. This tribe lived along the Columbia River in southern Washington. They spoke the Penutian language, and their name in their native tongue means "runaway."

Stage Names, Pen Names, and Other Famous Pseudonyms

■

For years, it's been the vogue for famous people to use pseudonyms and stage names, often because the real name may have been too cumbersome or difficult to remember. And a few hundred years ago, the theater was looked down upon, so prominent people worked under false names to protect their families' reputations. William Sidney Porter, however, used the name O. Henry to conceal his jail record. This chapter includes the names selected by entertainers, writers, and other famous people from a cross section of fields.

ACTORS MAKING A NAME FOR THEMSELVES

Here are the stage names of many well-known actors as well as their given names.

Nick Adams	Nicholas Adamshock
Joey Adams	Joseph Abramowitz
Anouk Aimee	Françoise Sorya
Eddie Albert	Edward Albert Heimberger
Alan Alda	Alphonse D'Abruzzo

Woody Allen	Allen Stewart Konigsberg
June Allyson	Ella Geisman
Don Ameche	Dominic Felix Amici
Andre the Giant	Andre Roussimoff
Julie Andrews	Julia Elizabeth Wells
Ann-Margret	Ann Margret Olsson
Eve Arden	Eunice Quedens
James Arness	James Aurness
Desi Arnaz	Desiderio Albert Arnaz de Acha III
Beatrice Arthur	Bernice Frankel
Fred Astaire	Frederick Austerlitz
Mary Astor	Lucille Vasconcells Langhanke
Charles Atlas	Angelo Siciliano
Lauren Bacall	Betty Joan Perske
Lucille Ball	Dianne Belmont
Anne Bancroft	Annemarie Louisa Italiano
Brigitte Bardot	Camille Javal
Ethel Barrymore	Ethel Mae Blythe
Lionel Barrymore	Lionel Blythe
Orson Bean	Dallas Frederick Burrows
Warren Beatty	Henry Warren Beaty
Jack Benny	Benjamin Kubelsky
Polly Bergen	Nellie Paulina Burgin
Busby Berkeley	William Berkeley Enos
Robbie Benson	Robert Segal
Milton Berle	Milton Berlinger
Irving Berlin	Israel Baline
Sarah Bernhardt	Rosine Bernard
Robert Blake	Michael Gubitosi
Nellie Bly	Elizabeth Cochrane Seaman
Shirley Booth	Thelma Booth Ford
Fannie Brice	Fanny Borach
Charles Bronson	Charles Buchinsky
Albert Brooks	Albert Einstein
Mel Brooks	Melvin Kaminsky
George Burns	Nathan Birnbaum

Raymond Burr	William Stacey Burr
Ellen Burstyn	Edna Rae Gillooly
Richard Burton	Richard Walter Jenkins
Red Buttons	Aaron Chwatt
Michael Caine	Maurice Joseph Micklewhite
Rory Calhoun	Francis Timothy Durgin
Dyan Cannon	Samille Diane Friesen
Eddie Cantor	Edward Israel Itzkowitz
Judy Carne	Joyce Botterill
Vikki Carr	Florence Bisenta de Casillas Martinez Cardona
Diahann Carroll	Carol Diahann Johnson
Hopalong Cassidy	William Lawrence Boyd
Lon Chaney, Jr.	Creighton Chaney
Cyd Charisse	Tula Elice Finklea
Chevy Chase	Cornelius Crane Chase
Lee J. Cobb	Lee Jacob
Claudette Colbert	Lily Claudette Chauchoin
Gary Cooper	Frank James Cooper
David Copperfield	David Kotkin
Howard Cosell	Howard Cohen
Lou Costello	Louis Cristillo
Joan Crawford	Lucille Le Sueur, then Billie Cassin
Tom Cruise	Thomas Cruise Mopother IV
Constance Cummings	Constance Halverstadt
Tony Curtis	Bernard Schwartz
Vic Damone	Vito Farinola
Rodney Dangerfield	Jacob Cohen
Doris Day	Doris Kappelhoff
Yvonne DeCarlo	Peggy Yvonne Middleton
Ruby Dee	Ruby Ann Wallace
Sandra Dee	Alexandra Zuck
Bo Derek	Mary Cathleen Collins
Angie Dickinson	Angeline Brown
Marlene Dietrich	Marie Magdalene Dietrich
Phyllis Diller	Phyllis Driver

Troy Donahue	Merle Johnson
Kirk Douglas	Issur Danielovitch Demsky
Patty Duke	Anne Marie Duke
Dale Evans	Frances Octavia Smith
Nanette Fabray	Ruby Bernadette Nanette Fabares
Douglas Fairbanks	Douglas Elton Ulman
Morgan Fairchild	Patsy Ann McClenny
Mia Farrow	Maria de Lourdes Villiers Farrow
Jose Ferrer	Jose Vincente Ferrer Otero y Cintron
Gracie Fields	Grace Stansfield
W. C. Fields	William Claude Dukinfield
Joan Fontaine	Joan de Havilland
Margot Fonteyn	Margaret Hookham
John Ford	Sean O'Fearna
Jodie Foster	Alicia Christian Foster
Redd Foxx	John Elroy Sanford
Kay Francis	Katherine Gibbs
Zsa Zsa Gabor	Sari Gabor
Greta Garbo	Greta Louisa Gustafsson
Ava Gardner	Lucy Johnson
John Garfield	Julius Garfinkle
Judy Garland	Frances Gumm
James Garner	James Baumgarner
Mitzi Gaynor	Francesca Mitzi Marlene de Czanyi von Gerber
Ben Gazzara	Biago Anthony Gazzara
Lillian Gish	Lillian de Guiche
Whoopi Goldberg	Caryn Johnson
Ruth Gordon	Ruth Gordon Jones
Elliot Gould	Elliot Goldstein
Stewart Granger	Jimmy Stewart
Cary Grant	Archibald Alexander Leach
Peter Graves	Peter Aurness
Joel Grey	Joe Katz
Buddy Hackett	Leonard Hacker
Jean Harlow	Harlean Carpenter

Rex Harrison	Reginald Carey Harrison
Laurence Harvey	Larushka Mischa Skikne
Sterling Hayden	John Hamilton
Gabby Hayes	George Francis Hayes
Helen Hayes	Helen Hayes Brown
Rita Hayworth	Margarita Cansino
Susan Hayward	Edythe Marriner
Audrey Hepburn	Edda Hepburn van Heemstra
Pee Wee Herman	Paul Rubenfeld, Paul Reubens
William Holden	William Franklin Beedle
Judy Holliday	Judith Tuvim
Bob Hope	Leslie Townes Hope
Harry Houdini	Ehrich Weiss
Leslie Howard	Leslie Stainer
Rock Hudson	Roy Scherer, Jr., Roy Harold Fitzgerald
Tab Hunter	Arthur Andrew Gelien
Walter Huston	Walter Houghston
Betty Hutton	Betty Thornburg
Burl Ives	Burl Icle Ivanhoe
Don Johnson	Donald Wayne
Al Jolson	Asa Yoelson
Jennifer Jones	Phyllis Isley
Boris Karloff	William Henry Pratt
Danny Kaye	David Daniel Kaminski
Diane Keaton	Diane Hall
Buster Keaton	Joseph Francis Keaton
Michael Keaton	Michael Douglas
Larry King	Lawrence Harvey Zeiper
Ben Kingsley	Krishna Banji
Nastassia Kinski	Nastassja Nakszybski
Cheryl Ladd	Cheryl Stoppelmoor
Veronica Lake	Constance Ockleman
Hedy Lamarr	Hedwig Kiesler
Dorothy Lamour	Dorothy Kaumeyer
Ann Landers	Esther Pauline Friedman
Michael Landon	Eugene Michael Orowitz

Stan Laurel	Arthur Stanley Jefferson
Bruce Lee	Lee Yuen Kam
Peggy Lee	Norma Dolores Egstrom
Vivian Leigh	Vivian Mary Hartley
Jerry Lewis	Joseph Levitch
Shari Lewis	Shari Hurwitz
Hal Linden	Harold Lipschitz
Carole Lombard	Carole Jane Peters
Sophia Loren	Sofia Scicolone
Peter Lorre	Lazlo Lowenstein
Myrna Loy	Myrna Williams
Shirley MacLaine	Shirley Beaty
Karl Malden	Malden Sekulovich
Jayne Mansfield	Vera Jayne Palmer
Frederic March	Frederick Bickel
E. G. Marshall	Edda Gunnar Marshall
Dean Martin	Dino Crocetti
Chico Marx	Leonard Marx
Groucho Marx	Julius Marx
Gummo Marx	Milton Marx
Harpo Marx	Adolph Marx
Zeppo Marx	Herbert Marx
Jackie Mason	Jacob Masler
Walter Matthau	Walter Matuschanskayasky
Virginia Mayo	Virginia May Jones
Steve McQueen	Terence Stephen McQueen
Vera Miles	Vera May Ralston
Ray Milland	Reginald Truscott-Jones
Ann Miller	Lucille Ann Collier
Carmen Miranda	Maria da Carmo Mirando de Cunha
Marilyn Monroe	Norma Jean Baker
Yves Montand	Ivo Livi
George Montgomery	George Montgomery Letz
Demi Moore	Demi Gynes
Zero Mostel	Samuel Joel Mostel
Paul Muni	Muni Weisenfreund

Mike Nichols	Michael Igor Peschowsky
Kim Novak	Marilyn Novak
Merle Oberon	Estelle Merle O'Brien Thompson
Margaret O'Brien	Angela Maxine O'Brien
Maureen O'Hara	Maureen Fitzsimmons
Jack Palance	Walter Jack Palanuik
Bernadette Peters	Bernadette Lazzaro
Mary Pickford	Gladys Mary Smith
Slim Pickens	Louis Lindley
Jane Powell	Suzanne Burce
Stefanie Powers	Stefanie Zofra Federkiewicz
Paula Prentiss	Paula Ragusa
Priscilla Presley	Priscilla Wagner Beaulieu
George Raft	George Ranft
Sally Rand	Helen Beck
Tony Randall	Leonard Rosenberg
Martha Raye	Margaret Teresa Yvonne O'Reed
Nancy Reagan	Anne Frances Robbins
Debbie Reynolds	Mary Frances Reynolds
Joan Rivers	Joan Sandra Molinsky
Ginger Rogers	Virginia Katharine McMath
Roy Rogers	Leonard Slye
Mickey Rooney	Joe Yule, Jr.
Soupy Sales	Milton Hines
Susan Sarandon	Susan Tomaling
Telly Savalas	Aristotle Savalas
Romy Schneider	Rosemarie Albach-Retty
Lizabeth Scott	Emma Matzo
Jane Seymour	Joyce Frankenberg
Omar Sharif	Michael Shalhoub
Martin Sheen	Ramon Estevez
Talia Shire	Talia Coppola
Phil Silvers	Philip Silversmith
Red Skelton	Richard Skelton
Suzanne Somers	Suzanne Mahoney
Elke Sommer	Elke Schletz

Sissy Spacek	Mary Elizabeth Spacek
Kim Stanley	Patricia Kimberly Reid
Meryl Streep	Mary Louise Streep
Barry Sullivan	Patrick Barry
Max von Sydow	Carl Adolf von Sydow
Robert Taylor	Spangler Arlington Brough
Terry-Thomas	Thomas Terry Hoar-Stevens
Danny Thomas	Amos Jacobs
Mike Todd	Avrom Hirsch Goldbogen
Rip Torn	Elmore Rual Torn, Jr.
Lana Turner	Julia Turner
Rudolph Valentino	Rudolpho Alfonzo Raffaelo Pierre Filibert Guglielmo di Valentina D'Antonguolla
Rudy Vallee	Hubert Prior Vallee
Erich von Stroheim	Hans Erich Maria Stroheim von Nordenwall
Nancy Walker	Ann Myrtle Swoyer
Warner Brothers (producers)	Albert, Harry, Jack, and Samuel Eichelbaum
John Wayne	Marion Michael Morrison
Clifton Webb	Webb Parmelee Hollenbeck
Tuesday Weld	Susan Ker Weld
Gene Wilder	Jerry Silberman
Natalie Wood	Natasha Gurdin
Shelley Winters	Shirley Schrift
Jane Wyman	Sarah Jane Fulks
Gig Young	Byron Barr
Loretta Young	Gretchen Jung

MUSICAL ENTERTAINERS

The following entertainers in the music field have changed their names, though some of the names sounded more "musical" before the change!

Pat Benatar	Patricia Andrzejewski
Tony Bennett	Anthony Benedetto
Irving Berlin	Israel Baline
Eubie Blake	James Hubert
Victor Borge	Borge Rosenbaum
David Bowie	David Robert Jones
Boy George	George O'Dowd
Maria Callas	Maria Kalogeropolos
Ray Charles	Ray Charles Robinson
Chubby Checker	Ernest Evans
Nat King Cole	Nathaniel Adams Coles
Alice Cooper	Vincent Furnier
Elvis Costello	Declan McManus
Bing Crosby	Harry Lillis Crosby
Bobby Darin	Robert Cassotto
Jimmy Dean	Seth Ward
John Denver	Henry John Deutchendorf, Jr.
Johnny Desmond	Giovanni de Simone
Bo Diddley	Ellas McDaniel
Fats Domino	Antoine Domino
Bob Dylan	Robert Zimmerman
Duke Ellington	Edward Kennedy Ellington
"Mama" Cass Elliot	Ellen Naomi Cohen
Freddie Fender	Baldemar Huerta
Connie Francis	Concetta Franconero
Crystal Gayle	Brenda Gayle Webb
Bobbie Gentry	Roberta Streeter
Dizzy Gillespie	John Birks Gillespie
Bill Haley	William John Clifton Haley, Jr.
M. C. Hammer	Stanley Kirk Burrell

133

■

How Some Popular Bands Were Named

Just as entertainers come up with interesting stage names, so do musical groups. Here are the stories of how some of the most famous musical groups were named:

Beatles. This name was inspired by Buddy Holly's group, the Crickets.

The Doors. This name was inspired by a line from a William Blake poem: "If the doors of perception were cleansed/All things would appear infinite."

Duran Duran. This group got its name from a villain in the Jane Fonda film *Barbarella*.

Led Zeppelin. Keith Moon (of the Rolling Stones) named *Led Zeppelin* after saying the group would never get off the ground.

Lynyrd Skynyrd. This group, which was formed as a high-school trio, was named for a strict PE teacher, Leonard Skinner.

Pink Floyd. This band's name was inspired by Georgia bluesmen Pink Anderson and Floyd Council.

The Rolling Stones. The group named itself after a Muddy Waters blues song.

Steely Dan. The group got its name from a William S. Burroughs novel.

The Turtles. This U.S. band was named to cash in on a British-sounding name such as *The Beatles*.

U2. This name was chosen to imply that every fan in the audience could join in with the music as well.

UB40. This group named itself *UB40* because most of the members at the time were unemployed, so they took the name from their unemployment benefit forms.

The Who. The band started off as the *Detours* but changed to *The Who* after seeing another band called *Detours* on TV.

Skitch Henderson	Lyle Russell Cedric Henderson
Billie Holiday	Eleonora Fagan
Engelbert Humperdinck	Arnold Dorsey
Billy Idol	William Board
Elton John	Reginald Kenneth Dwight
Tom Jones	Thomas Jones Woodward
Gypsy Rose Lee	Rose Louise Hovick
Julie London	Julie Peck
Loretta Lynn	Loretta Webb
Tony Martin	Alvin Morris
Meat Loaf	Marvin Lee Aday
Dame Nellie Melba	Helen Porter Mitchell
Ethel Merman	Ethel Zimmerman
Joni Mitchell	Roberta Joan Anderson
Jelly Roll Morton	Ferdinand Joseph La Menthe
Jacques Offenbach	Jacob Eberst
Patti Page	Clara Ann Fowler
Minnie Pearl	Sarah Ophelia Colley Cannon
Roberta Peters	Roberta Peterman
Edith Piaf	Edith Gassion
Della Reese	Deloreese Patricia Early
Bobby Rydell	Robert Riderelli
Artie Shaw	Abraham Isaac Arshawsky
Beverly Sills	Belle "Bubbles" Miriam Silverman
Nina Simone	Eunice Kathleen Waymon
Ringo Starr	Richard Starkey
Cat Stevens	Steven Georgion
Connie Stevens	Concetta Ingolia

Franz von Suppe	Francisco Ezechiele Eermeegildo Suppe Demelli
Tiny Tim	Herbert Khaury
Tina Turner	Annie Mae Bullock
Conway Twitty	Harold Lloyd Jenkins
Bruno Walter	Bruno Walter Schlesinger
Dionne Warwick	Marie Dionne Warrick
Muddy Waters	McKinley Morganfield
Hank Williams, Sr.,	Hiram King Williams
Stevie Wonder	Steveland Morris
Tammy Wynette	Wynette Pugh

WRITERS' PEN NAMES

Long before authors went on tour and appeared on radio and television talk shows to sell their wares, they used pen names primarily to hide their true identity. Here are some pen names of famous authors.

Pen Name	Author
Shalom Aleichem	Sholem Yakov Rabinowitz
Max Brand	Gerald Kenneth Tierney
Pearl Buck	Pearl Comfort Sydenstricker
Anthony Burgess	John Anthony Burgess Wilson
Taylor Caldwell	Janet Taylor Caldwell
Truman Capote	Truman Streckfus Persons
Lewis Carroll	Charles Lutwidge Dodgson
Agatha Christie	Agatha Mary Clarissa Miller
Joseph Conrad	Teodor J. Konrad Korzeniowski
Isak Dinesen	Baroness Karen Blixen
George Eliot	Mary Ann Evans
O. Henry	William Sydney Porter
James Herriot	James Alfred Wight
Victoria Holt	Eleanor Burford Hibbert

Michael Innes	I. M. Stewart
Judith Krantz	Judith Tarcher
John Le Carre	David John Moore Cornwell
Molière	Jean Baptiste Poquelin
George Orwell	Eric Arthur Blair
Dorothy Parker	Dorothy Rothschild
George Sand	Aurore Lucie Dudevant
Dr. Seuss	Theodore Seuss Geisel
Tom Stoppard	Thomas Straussler
Mark Twain	Samuel Langhorne Clemens
Gore Vidal	Eugene Luther Vidal
Voltaire	François Marie Arouet
Nathanael West	Nathan Wallenstien Weinstein
Tennessee Williams	Thomas Lanier Williams

FAMOUS WRITERS WHO HAVE USED LESS WELL KNOWN PEN NAMES

In some cases, writers whose names have become well known use a pseudonym, sometimes to protect their identity, sometimes to write in a different style. Here are some famous writers who have written under lesser-known names.

Author	**Pen Name**
Kingsley Amis	Robert Markham
Charlotte Brontë	Currer Bell
Harlan Ellison	Lee Archer
Erle Stanley Gardner	A. A. Fair
Stephen King	Richard Bachman
Joyce Carol Oates	Rosamund Smith
Rosamunde Pilcher	Jane Fraser
Gore Vidal	Edgar Box
Anne Rice	A. N. Roquelaure, Anne Rampling

FAMOUS AMERICAN LEGENDS
AND THEIR REAL NAMES

The names of some of our most legendary characters are based on real people.

Johnny Appleseed. It was really John Chapman who planted apple trees from the Alleghenies westward.

Billy the Kid. This famous bandit of the southwest was actually William H. Bonney.

Buffalo Bill. This well-known frontiersman and showman was actually William Frederick Cody.

Butch Cassidy. The real name of this famous American outlaw was Robert LeRoy Parker.

Calamity Jane. This famous cowgirl was in real life Martha Jane Burke.

Crazy Horse. This Sioux leader's real name was Tashunca-Uitco.

Captain Kidd. This pirate's real name was William Kidd.

Pocahontas. Her actual name was Matoaka.

Sitting Bull. This Dakota Sioux chief's name was Tatanka Iyotake.

Sundance Kid. The real name of Butch Cassidy's sidekick was Harry Longbaugh.

STILL MORE FAMOUS AND INFAMOUS PEOPLE WHO CHANGED THEIR NAMES

"Legs" Diamond	John T. Nolana
Rocky Graziano	Tom Barbelo
Adolf Hitler	Adolph Schicklgruber
Nikolai Lenin	Vladimir Ilich Ulyanov
Rocky Marciano	Rocco Marchegiano
Kid McCoy	Norman Selby
Sugar Ray Robinson	Walker Smith
Joseph Stalin	Iosif V. Dzhugashvili

Mati Hari

Mata Hari was the famous World War I spy who wooed high-ranking officers of the Allied and German armies while apparently spying for both sides. Born in Leeuwarden, Netherlands, as *Margaretha Geertruide Zelle* in 1876, she left this town at the age of 19 and married a captain in the Royal Dutch East Indies Army. The young bride accompanied her husband to Indonesia, the former Dutch colony, where their relation quickly soured. In 1903, she left him and went to Paris where she began dancing in nightclubs and nude reviews. As her stage name, she chose *Mata Hari*, Japanese for "eye of the morning." Mata Hari's sense of adventure led her to become involved with men in the most powerful circles and brought her prized military secrets. Consequently, both the French and the Germans reportedly enlisted her as a spy. But in time, the French army became suspicious and eventually executed her in the Paris suburb of Vincennes in October 1917. Mata Hari insisted on wearing her trademark black silk stockings while facing the firing squad.

The All-Time Baddest Bad Guys

Many of the all-time worst villains in American crime had colorful nicknames. Here are a few of them:

Frank "The Dasher" Abbandando
Tony "Joe Batters" Accardo
Joseph "Ha Ha" Aiuppa
Israel "Icepick Willie" Alderman
Louis "Pretty" Amberg
Michael "Umbrella Mike" Boyle
Louis "Lepke" Buchalter
Al "Scarface" Capone
Vincent "Mad Dog" Coll
Jack "Legs" Diamond
Joseph "Joe Adonis" Doto
Joseph "Diamond Joe" Esposito
Charles "Pretty Boy" Floyd
Charlie "Monkey Face" Genker
Jake "Greasy Thumb" Guzik
William "Billy" Hill
"Golf Bag" Sam Hunt
Alvin "Creepy" Karpis
George "Machine Gun" Kelly
Charles "Lucky" Luciano
Jack "Machine Gun" McGurn
Thomas "Butterfingers" Moran
Lester "Baby Face" Nelson
Benjamin "Bugsy" Siegel

A Writer with Many Names

Frank Stratemeyer assumed many pseudonyms for the different series of books that he penned. Stratemeyer wrote under the name of Franklin W. Dixon for his famous *Hardy Boys* series, and for the *Tom Swift* series, he used the name Victor Appleton. Then, when Stratemeyer wrote for a different market—young girls—he assumed female names. For his popular *Bobbsey Twins* series, he was Laura Lee Hope, and for the best-selling *Nancy Drew* mysteries, Stratemeyer became Carolyn Keene.

SOME FAMOUS REAL NAMES

While many writers and entertainers change their names for a variety of reasons, some keep their given names. Here are some real names that sound as if they were made up.

Paul Anka	Bradford Dillman
Tallulah Bankhead	Clint Eastwood
Harry Belafonte	Nelson Eddy
Candice Bergen	Marianne Faithfull
Ingrid Bergman	Errol Flynn
Humphrey Bogart	Jane Fonda
Clara Bow	Art Garfunkel
Marlon Brando	Greer Garson
Hoagy Carmichael	Zane Grey
Primo Carnera	Goldie Hawn
Johnny Cash	Alfred Hitchcock
Charlie Chaplin	Dustin Hoffman
Noel Coward	Celeste Holm
Olivia de Havilland	Jimmy Jewell
Neil Diamond	Gene Kelly

Eartha Kitt	Anthony Quinn
Kris Kristofferson	Burt Reynolds
Jack Lemmon	Cesar Romero
Gina Lollobrigida	Damon Runyon
Mercedes	Frank Sinatra
McCambridge	Rod Steiger
Barry Manilow	Rod Stewart
Melina Mercouri	Barbra Streisand
Roger Moore	Mel Torme
Derek Nimmo	Spencer Tracy
Walter Pidgeon	Ben Turpin
Cole Porter	King Vidor
Tyrone Power	Mae West
Elvis Presley	Frank Zappa

PEOPLE'S NAMES IN SONG

The following is a list of first names that have been immortalized by appearing in song titles:

Adeline	"Sweet Adeline"
Alexander	"Alexander's Ragtime Band"
Alfie	"Alfie"
Alice	"Sweet Alice"; "Alice's Restaurant"
Allison	"Allison"
Angie	"Angie"; "Angie Baby"
Annie	"Annie Laurie"; "Annie's Song" *Annie* (the musical)
Betsy	"Sweet Betsy from Pike"
Bill	"Bill Bailey, Won't You Please Come Home?"; "Steamboat Bill"; "Won't You Marry Me Bill . . ."
Billy	"Billy Boy"
Billy Jean	"Billy Jean"
Bobby	"Bobby Shaftoe"; "I Want to be Bobby's Girl"; "Me and Bobby McGee"

Famous People Better Known by Their Middle Names

George Edward *Eddie* Arcaro, jockey
Yitzak *Ed* Asner, actor
Orvon *Gene* Autry, actor
Henry *Warren* Beatty, actor
Francis *Lee* Bailey, attorney
Ernest *Ingmar* Bergman, film director
James Hubert *Eubie* Blake, musician
Charles Eugene *Pat* Boone, singer
Edmund Gerald *"Jerry"* Brown, governor (California)
George *Richard* Chamberlain, actor
Edward *Montgomery* Clift, actor
Alfred *Alistair* Cooke, author/historian
Morris *Mac* Davis, musician
Ruth Elizabeth *Bette* Davis, actress
Mary *Farrah* Fawcett, actress
William *Clark* Gable, actor
Herbert John *Jackie* Gleason, actor
Charles *Van* Johnson, actor
Alice *"Ali"* McGraw, actress
Terence Stephen *"Steve"* McQueen, actor
George Robert *"Bob"* Newhart, actor
Patrick *Ryan* O'Neal, actor
Olive *Marie* Oswald, singer
Margaret *Jane* Pauley, television commentator
Eldred *Gregory* Peck, actor
David Samuel *"Sam"* Peckinpah, film director
Ernestine *Jane* Russell, actress
Charles *Robert* Redford, actor
Lynn *Nolan* Ryan, baseball pitcher
Christa *Brooke* Shields, actress
Marvin *Neil* Simon, playwright
Michael *Sylvester* Stallone, actor
Mary Jean *Lily* Thomas, actress

Myron *Mike* Wallace, television commentator
George *Orson* Welles, actor
Walter *Bruce* Willis, actor
Mary *Debra* Winger, actress

Famous People with One Name

There are a handful of people who are so well known, they go by only one name. Here are some of these one-named luminaries and their real names:

Cantinflas	Mario Moreno August
Capucine	Germaine Lefebvre
Charo	Mario Rosario Pilar/Martinez Melina Baeza
Cher	Cher Sarkesian (later Cher La Piere)
Dagmar	Dion Di Mucci
Fabian	Fabian Anthony Forte
Heloise*	Heloise Bowles Reese
Heloise	Ponce Kiah Marchelle Heloise Cruise (daughter)
Hildegarde	Hildegarde Loretta Sell
Kreskin	George Joseph Kresge, Jr.
Liberace	Wladziu Valentino Liberace
Madonna	Madonna Louise Veronica Ciccone
Malcolm X	Malcolm Little
Pelé	Edson Arantes do Nascimento
Prince	Prince Rogers Nelson
Rasputin	Grigori Efimovich
Sting	Gordon Matthew Sumner
Tito	Josip Broz
Twiggy	Leslie Hornby

*After the death of her mother, who was the first Heloise, Cruise became the writer of the Heloise column.

144

Bonnie	"My Bonnie Lies Over the Ocean"
Brian	"Brian's Song"
Caroline	"Sweet Caroline"
Casey	"Casey Jones"
Cathy	"Cathy's Clown"
Charlie	"Charlie Is My Darling"
Charlotte	"Hush Hush, Sweet Charlotte"
Chuck	"Chuck E.'s in Love"
Clementine	"My Darling Clementine"
Daisy	"Daisy Bell (A Bicycle Built for Two)"
Dan	"Old Dan Tucker"
Daniel	"Daniel"
Danny	"Danny Deever"; "Danny Boy"
Diana	"Diana"
Dinah	"Dinah"
Dolly	"Hello, Dolly!"
Ezekiel	"Ezekiel Saw the Wheel"
Frankie	"Frankie and Johnny"
Georgia	"Sweet Georgia Brown"; "Georgia on My Mind"
Guinevere	"Guinevere"
Harry	"I'm Just Wild About Harry"
Hernando	"Hernando's Hideaway"
Irene	"Irene" (from *Irene*); "Good Night, Irene"
Jack	"Jack and Jill"; "Little Jack Horner"; "Hit the Road Jack"
James	"Sweet Baby James"
Jane	"The Death of Queen Jane"
Jean	"Jean"
Jeanie	"Jeanie with the Light Brown Hair"
Jill	"Jack and Jill"
Johnny	"When Johnny Comes Marching Home"; "Frankie and Johnny"; "Johnny Get Your Gun"; "Oh, Johnny, Oh, Johnny, Oh!"; "Johnny One Note"
Josephine, Jo	"Josephine, My Jo"
Joshua	"Joshua Fit the Battle of Jericho"
Juanita	"Juanita"

145

Jude	"Hey Jude"
Judy	"Suite: Judy Blue Eyes"; "Judy, Judy, Judy, Do You Love Me?"
Julie	"When Julie Comes Around"
Kathleen	"Kathleen Mavourneen"; "I'll Take You Home Again, Kathleen"
Lara	"Lara's Theme (Somewhere My Love)"
Layla	"Layla"
Leroy	"Bad, Bad Leroy Brown"
Lili	"Lili Marlene"
Liza Jane	"Good-bye, Liza Jane"; "Li'l Liza Jane"
Lorraine	"Sweet Lorraine"
Lou	"Skip to My Lou"
Louis	"Meet Me in St. Louis, Louis"
Lucy	"Lucy in the Sky with Diamonds"
Lulu	"Lulu's Back in Town"
Madeline	"Paddlin' Madelin' Home"
Maggie	"When You and I Were Young, Maggie"
Mandy	"Mandy"
Margery	"Seesaw, Margery Daw"
Maria	"Maria" (from *West Side Story*); "Maria" (from *The Sound of Music*)
Marlene	"Lili Marlene"
Mary	"Oh, Mary, Don't You Weep, Don't You Mourn"; "Mary Had a Little Lamb"; "Mary's a Grand Old Name"; "Proud Mary"
Mary Ann	"Mary Ann"
Matilda	"Waltzing Matilda"
Michael	"Michael Rowed the Boat Ashore"
Michelle	"Michelle"
Mona	"Mona Lisa"
Moses	"Go Down, Moses"
Ned	"(Old) Uncle Ned"
Nellie, Nelly	"Nelly Bly"; "Nelly Was a Lady"; "When I Saw Sweet Nellie Home"
Norma Jean	"Goodbye Norma Jean"

146

Pearl	"My Pearl's a Bowery Girl"
Peg	"Peg o' My Heart"; "Peg"
Peggy	"Peggy"; "Peggy Sue"
Peter	"Peter, Peter Pumpkin-Eater"
Polly	"Polly, Put the Kettle On"
Ramona	"Ramona"
Rhonda	"Help Me, Rhonda"
Rikki	"Rikki Don't Lose That Number"
Ron	"Da Doo Ron Ron"
Rose	"Honeysuckle Rose"
Rose Marie	"Rose Marie"
Rosie	"Sweet Rosie O'Grady"
Sally	"Lay Down Sally"
Sandra	"Look at Me, I'm Sandra Dee"
Sara	"Sara Smile"
Sheila	"Tequila Sheila"
Sherry	"Sherry"
Simon	"Simple Simon"
Sue	"I Love You in the Same Old Way, Darling Sue"; "Sweet Sue (Just You)"; "A Boy Named Sue"; "Runaround Sue"
Susanna	"O, Susanna"
Susie	"If You Knew Susie, Like I Know Susie"; "Wake Up Little Susie"; "Susie Q"
Tom	"Tom Tom, the Piper's Son"; "Tom Dooley"
Venus	"Venus" "Venus in Blue Jeans"

147

Nicknames of College Teams

—— ■ ——

Did you ever wonder how certain U.S. college teams got their nicknames? Some students make it through their college years not knowing how their school team got nicknamed. For instance, why is the team from Arkansas University nicknamed the *Razorbacks* or the one from Purdue University the *Boilermakers?* This chapter reveals how the teams of many schools in America got nicknamed.

University of Alabama at Tuscaloosa. The athletes of the university of Alabama were given the nickname the *Crimson Tide* by a sports editor of the *Birmingham News* because the team's colors are crimson and white.

University of Alabama at Birmingham. The University of Alabama teams were nicknamed the *Blazers* in 1978 to symbolize the fact that the fast-growing college "is blazing its way into history."

University of Alaska at Anchorage. The teams at the University of Alaska were given the nickname the *Seawolves* in 1977 in honor of a mythical sea creature in Alaska that had a wolf's head and a whale's tale.

MICHAEL D. SHOOK

University of Alaska at Fairbanks. The male teams of the University of Alaska are nicknamed the *Nanooks*, meaning "polar bear" in the Inqupiaq Eskimo language. The women's teams are called the *Lady Nanooks*.

Albion College. Since Albion is another name for England, the nickname the *Britons* is well suited to the athletic teams of this Michigan school.

Allegheny College. Allegheny College in Meadville, Pennsylvania, adopted the nickname the *Alligators* for its teams in the late 1920s because Allegheny *Alligators* sounded too good to pass up.

American University. The U.S. Congress created American University in 1893 in the nation's capital. Its team colors are red, white, and blue, and it seemed only natural to call the school teams the *Eagles*. The bald eagle, America's national bird is the school mascot.

Amherst College. Amherst College teams are nicknamed *Lord Jeffs* and *Lady Jeffs* after Lord Jeffrey Amherst, a British war hero of the eighteenth-century French and Indian War. This Massachusetts town was named for Lord Amherst and the college was named for the town and its people, who spent much time and effort building the school.

Arizona State University. There are two explanations for why Arizona State University athletes are called the *Sun Devils*. Some say it stemmed from a university booster group called the "Sun Angels." Others say it came from Donn Kinzle, a former athletic director who was a Duke University *Blue Devil* as an undergraduate.

University of Arizona. The University of Arizona teams inherited their nickname the *Wildcats* following an Arizona-

150

Occidental football game. Bill Henry, a writer for the *Los Angeles Times*, wrote, "The Arizona men showed the fight of wildcats," and the name caught on.

Arkansas State University. Athletes at Arkansas State University were nicknamed the *Indians* because of the fighting spirit of the Osage Indians who roamed Northern Arkansas during the eighteenth century and fought practically all other tribes there.

University of Arkansas at Fayetteville. The University of Arkansas nicknamed its teams the *Razorbacks* in 1909. After beating LSU in Memphis 16–1, coach Hugo Bezdek referred to his players as "a wild team of razorback hogs." The team previously had been called the *Cardinals*.

University of Arkansas at Little Rock. The University of Arkansas called its teams the *Trojans* in 1931 after the players and coach took a vote on a nickname for the new basketball team. They wanted something that would illustrate their aggressiveness, so a student suggested the Trojan Horse, hence the Trojans.

Auburn University. Originally, this school in Auburn, Alabama, was known as Alabama Polytechnic Institute. In 1895, its football team received the nickname the *Auburn Tigers* because their orange and black stockings suggested the stripes of a tiger.

Ball State University. Players at Ball State University at Muncie, Indiana, were called the *Hoosieroons* until 1927 when the administration, students, and coaches tired of the name and wanted a change. A contest was held and coach Paul "Billy" Williams, a loyal fan of the St. Louis Cardinals, proposed the *Cardinals*. It won by a landslide.

151

Bates College. Athletes at Bates College, in Lewiston, Maine, were nicknamed the *Bobcats* in 1922 after a search was launched for a team mascot. An alumnus chose this animal because it is a native of Maine's woods and because a bobcat has an "unlimited determination and fighting spirit."

Baylor University. Teams from Baylor University of Waco, Texas, inherited the nickname the *Bears* in the late 1920s after a student found a bear on the steps of an old drug store abandoned there by a traveling circus. The enterprising student worked out a deal with the university's president: He offered to take care of the bear as the school's mascot in exchange for free tuition.

Boise State University. Boise State University in Idaho chose the name the *Broncos* for its teams in 1964 because the bronco is symbolic of the spirit and determination of the wild horses that roam the Idaho wilderness.

Boston College. The nickname the *Eagles* was chosen for Boston College teams because eagles are known for their swiftness and strength, two winning qualities of superior athletes.

Boston State College. Boston State College chose the nickname the *Warriors* for its athletes in 1952 to symbolize the pride and courage that sports teams strive to possess.

Boston University. Boston University chose the nickname the *Terriers* for its teams in 1919 after choosing the Boston Terrier as its mascot. Interestingly, Boston University was incorporated in 1869, the same year the English Terrier was crossbred with the bulldog to create the Boston Terrier.

Bowdoin College. Athletes at Bowdoin College in Maine chose the *Polar Bear* as their mascot because of the school's active role in arctic exploration. In fact, in 1909 Rear Admiral Robert E. Peary of Bowdoin's class of 1877 became the first man to reach the North Pole, and the school has been called the *Explorer's College.*

Bowling Green State University. Bowling Green State University in Ohio adopted the name *Falcons* for its teams in 1927. The name was chosen by Ivan Lake, managing editor and sports editor of the *Bowling Green Sentinel Tribune*. He chose the name because it fit headline space well and because, he wrote "falcons were the most powerful bird for their size and often attacked birds two or three times their size."

Brandeis University. Teams at Brandeis University in Boston, Massachusetts, are nicknamed the *Judges* after the late Louis Dembitz Brandeis, associate justice of the Supreme Court, who served from 1916 to 1939. The school's mascot is the owl, which is a symbol of wise judgment and thoughtfulness.

Brigham Young University. After a search for a team nickname in the early 1920s, the *Cougars* was chosen for this school in Provo. The cougar is native to Utah and is powerful, agile, wise, and beautiful.

Brown University. Brown University in Providence, Rhode Island, inherited the nickname the *Bruins* for its athletes on January 20, 1904, when U.S. Senator Theodore Francis Green, class of 1887, picked the brown bear to be the school's mascot.

Bucknell University. Pennsylvania's Bucknell University picked the team nickname the *Bisons* in a reference to its

153

geography and history. Bucknell's campus is situated at the eastern end of the Buffalo Valley, which at one time was the stomping grounds of a huge herd of American buffalo or bison.

University of California at Berkeley. The University of California at Berkeley athletic teams are called the *Golden Bears* in honor of the California state flag, which features a grizzly bear on a green patch in the center of a white field.

University of California at Los Angeles (UCLA). The athletic teams at UCLA were nicknamed the *Bruins* in 1927 because the school began as a branch of the University of California at Berkeley, whose teams are called the Golden Bears. The first choice had been the *Grizzlies*, but it was already being used by the University of Montana.

University of California at San Diego. Teams at the University of California at San Diego were nicknamed the *Tritons* because of the school's proximity to the Pacific Ocean and its connections with the Scripps Institute of Oceanography.

Carnegie-Mellon University. Pittsburgh's Carnegie-Mellon University nicknamed its athletic teams the *Tartans* in the 1920s after Andrew Carnegie commissioned an Edinburgh weaver to design a tartan (a plaid textile design) for his family's exclusive use. In time, a similar design was seen brushing the knees of the Kiltie Band on the sidelines of football games.

University of Chicago. The University of Chicago athletic teams were nicknamed the *Maroons* because maroon was designated the school color on May 4, 1894.

Clemson University. Teams at Clemson University in South Carolina are nicknamed the *Tigers* for no particular reason. Perhaps it just sounded good.

Colby College. Athletic teams at Colby College were named the *White Mules* because they usually upset published predictions and were called the "dark horse." When Colby won the Maine state football championship in 1923, the name was changed to *White Mules*.

Colgate University. Sports teams at Colgate University in Hamilton, New York, were nicknamed the *Red Raiders* by sportswriter Dexter Teed, who referred to the football team one season as "the red raiders of the Chenango Valley."

Colorado State University. Colorado State University teams were nicknamed the *Rams* after the Rocky Mountain Bighorn Ram was adopted as the university's mascot in 1946.

University of Colorado at Boulder. The athletic teams at the University of Colorado are called the *Buffaloes* because the American Buffalo is native to Colorado.

Columbia University. The athletic teams at New York's Columbia University have been known as the *Lions* since 1910, when the school was presented with a blue and white banner bearing a lion with the motto "Leo Columbiae."

University of Connecticut. University of Connecticut teams were nicknamed the *Huskies* while the school was still called Connecticut State College. Tired of being known as the Aggies, the students voted to change the name to the Huskies in 1939.

155

Cornell University. Teams at Cornell University in Ithaca, New York, have been known as the *Big Red* since 1905 when alumnus Romeyn Berry wrote the lyrics for a new football song and referred to Cornell as the "big red team."

Dartmouth College. The athletic teams at Dartmouth College in Hanover, New Hampshire, are called the *Big Green* because the school colors are green and white.

University of Dayton. The University of Dayton nicknamed its team the *Flyers* in 1923 because Dayton, Ohio, is the home of aviation pioneers Orville and Wilbur Wright.

University of Delaware. The athletic teams at the University of Delaware in Wilmington are known as the *Fightin' Blue Hens* because Delaware is called the Blue Hen State.

Denison University. Teams at Denison University in Granville, Ohio, were nicknamed the *Big Red* by a sportswriter for the *Columbus Dispatch*. The name paid homage to a very successful Denison basketball team of the early 1920s, whose players were very tall and wore red uniforms.

University of Denver. The athletic teams at the University of Denver were nicknamed the *Pioneers* in 1927 by a vote of the student body because, "University of Denver is the pioneer institution of higher learning in the state of Colorado."

De Paul University. In 1900, when De Paul's first athletic teams were to represent the university, they had a big letter *D* monogrammed on their uniforms. Soon the Chicago college's teams were called *D-Men*, which eventually evolved to *Demons*. In 1901, the student body voted to change the name to *Blue Demons* because their colors were scarlet and royal blue.

156

De Pauw University. The athletic teams at De Pauw University in Greencastle, Indiana, were nicknamed the *Tigers* in 1918 because the team colors were black and gold and the name *Tigers* embodied a fighting spirit.

University of Detroit. The University of Detroit athletic teams were nicknamed the *Titans* in 1923 by Stan Brink, a sports reporter for the *Detroit Free Press*. He chose the name because the school's football players were so large they evoked images of the Titans of Greek mythology.

Drake University. Athletic teams at Iowa's Drake University were nicknamed the *Bulldogs* in 1909 by Art Gordon, a sports editor at the *Des Moines Register*. Gordon called the team "veritable bulldogs" because John L. Griffith, the head football coach at the time, had two bulldogs that he took everywhere.

Drew University. Since Drew University lies in a heavily wooded area in Madison, New Jersey, it had been known locally as the "forest." In 1955, when Drew needed a new athletic nickname, the *Rangers* was chosen (the forest *Rangers*).

Duke University. Athletic teams at Duke University in North Carolina were nicknamed the *Blue Devils* by William Lander and Mike Bradshaw, the editors of the school newspaper in 1922–1923. Tired of the previous nicknames, the *Methodists* and *Blue and White*, they chose *Blue Devils* instead.

Emory University. Emory University in Atlanta, Georgia, chose the nickname the *Eagles* for its athletic teams in 1950 because the American bald eagle is the national bird. The *Eagles* is the most popular nickname used at American colleges.

157

Florida State University. The athletic teams at Florida State University in Tallahassee were nicknamed the *Seminoles* in honor of the first Americans to inhabit the area.

University of Florida. Teams at the University of Florida in Gainesville were nicknamed the *Gators* by Phillip Miller, a Gainesville merchant who owned and operated a drugstore specializing in student goods. While ordering some team pennants and banners, Miller realized the university had no mascot. He chose an alligator because no other university had adopted it and the alligator was a native to the state.

Franklin College. This college in Franklin, Indiana, nicknamed its teams the *Grizzlies* after outstanding basketball coach Griz Wagner, who led the team in the 1920s.

Franklin & Marshall College. The athletic teams at Franklin & Marshall College in Lancaster, Pennsylvania, are nicknamed the *Diplomats* because the school is named after Benjamin Franklin and Chief Justice John Marshall.

Fresno State University. California's Fresno State University adopted the nickname the *Bulldogs* for its athletes in 1921. The student body president Warren Moody and friends were continually greeted by a white bulldog outside the main campus building. At a meeting, students decided to nickname the university teams for the friendly pooch.

George Washington University. Teams at George Washington University in Washington, D.C., are nicknamed the *Colonials* to honor the university namesake.

Georgetown University. The athletic teams at Georgetown University in the nation's capital are nicknamed the *Hoyas*, which originated as something of a joke. The university's baseball team was nicknamed the *Stonewalls* and one student, using Latin and Greek terms, dubbed them *Hoya Saxa*, which translates to "what rocks?" The name caught on and all Georgetown teams are now called *Hoyas*.

Georgia Institute of Technology (Georgia Tech). Georgia Tech in Atlanta has two nicknames for its sports teams. They are called the *Yellow Jackets* because the school colors are gold and white and they are referred to as the *Ramblin' Wreck* from a popular pep song that goes "I'm a ramblin' wreck from Georgia Tech."

University of Georgia. The University of Georgia in Athens nicknamed its teams the *Bulldogs* supposedly after Yale's *Bulldogs*. The University's first president, Abraham Baldwin, was a Yale alumnus. Many of the university's buildings, including Old College, were designed from the same blueprints used by Yale.

University of Hartford. Until the late 1940s, the University of Hartford in Connecticut was known as Hillyer College and the team nickname was the *Fighting Hawks*. When the University of Hartford was chartered, the nickname *Hawks* was kept, although its origin is unknown.

Hartwick College. The athletic teams at Hartwick College in Oneonta, New York, have been known since 1928 as the *Warriors*, a nickname implying their fierce nature.

Harvard University. Teams at Harvard University in Cambridge, Massachusetts, have had the nickname the *Crimsons* since that color was chosen as the school color by a meeting of undergraduates on May 6, 1875.

University of Hawaii. The athletic teams at Honolulu's University of Hawaii are nicknamed the *Rainbows* for the rainbows that are frequently seen in Manoa Valley, where the campus is located. The football team is nicknamed the *Rainbow Warriors* and the women's teams are called the *Rainbow Wahines*, a Hawaiian word for "women."

Holy Cross College. Sports teams at Holy Cross College in Worcester, Massachusetts, were nicknamed the *Crusaders* in 1925 by the student body in reference to the college's church-related heritage.

University of Houston. The teams at the University of Houston were nicknamed the *Cougars* in 1927 by a school committee that chose it from among the many nicknames suggested in the local newspapers.

Howard University. There are two theories about why athletic teams at Howard University in Washington, D.C., are called the *Bison*. The first suggests that *Bison* was a nickname Indians bequeathed to black regiments during the Indian Wars because the soldiers represented the best in fighting spirit (Howard is a predominately black university). The second theory claims it is because the bison is the symbol for the U.S. Department of the Interior, which at one time oversaw the university.

Humboldt State University. The athletic teams at Humboldt State University were nicknamed the *Lumberjacks* when the university was founded in 1913. The University is located in Humboldt County in Northern California, an area dominated by the timber industry.

Idaho State University. Teams at Idaho State University in Pocatello were nicknamed the *Bengals* in 1937 because the school colors were black and orange, the tiger's colors.

University of Idaho. University of Idaho athletic teams were nicknamed the *Vandals* by the sports editor of *The Argonaut,* the college paper, "because the spirit which pervades all Idaho intercollegiate activities is analogous to the spirit shown by the ancient Vandals in their fierce conquests" (Vandals were a Germanic people who wreaked havoc on Rome and other nations in the fourth and fifth centuries A.D.).

University of Illinois at Urbana-Champaign. The University of Illinois athletic teams were nicknamed the *Fighting Illini* in the early 1920s for the Illini Indians, who were known for their fighting spirit.

University of Illinois at Chicago. Athletes at the University of Illinois were nicknamed the *Flames* by a student vote because the campus is only three blocks from the site of the infamous Chicago fire of October 8, 1871.

Indiana University. The athletic teams of Indiana University are nicknamed the *Fightin' Hoosiers.* According to some, a *hoosier* is a rustic hill-dweller, named for his expression "Who's Yere?" when disturbed. Others say the term came from Sam Hoosier, a canal builder along the Ohio who hired many Indiana workers, known as Hoosier's men and later as Hoosiers.

Iowa State University. Iowa State University in Ames nicknamed its teams the *Cyclones* in 1895. That fall, a huge number of cyclones (tornadoes) tore through the state of Iowa. The morning after Iowa's football team beat Northwestern, the *Chicago Tribune* headlined the story "Iowa Cyclone Devastates Evanston."

University of Iowa. The athletic teams at the University of Iowa in Iowa City are nicknamed the *Hawkeyes* after the

161

state's nickname. There are two explanations for why Iowa is called the *Hawkeye State*. One says it was named for the Indian Chief Hawkeye, who terrorized travelers. The other says that Iowa was nicknamed after J. G. Edwards, also known as "Old Hawkeye." He was the editor of the *Burlington Patriot*, which was later named the *Hawkeye and Patriot*.

Ithaca College. Teams at Ithaca College in New York were nicknamed the *Bombers* in the late 1930s by Harold Jensen, a reporter from the *Ithaca Journal*. He nicknamed the football team after a huge win and the name stuck.

Kansas State University. The athletic teams at Kansas State University in Manhattan, Kansas, were nicknamed the *Wildcats* in 1915 by head football coach Chief Bender for their fighting spirit. The nickname was changed in 1916 to the *Farmers*, but Coach Charles Bachman switched it back to the *Wildcats* in 1920.

University of Kansas. The athletic teams at the University of Kansas, located in Lawrence, Kansas, are called the *Jayhawks*. The name is in reference to a *jayhawker*, a member of one of the bands of abolitionist guerillas that roved through Kansas and surrounding states during the Civil War. Ever since, people from Kansas have been referred to as Jayhawks, so the nickname was adopted by the state university, a school known for its powerhouse football and basketball teams.

Kent State University. Ohio's Kent State University nicknamed its teams the *Golden Flashes* in 1927 after president T. Howard Winters held a contest to replace the old nickname *Silver Foxes*. The person who suggested the *Golden Flashes* for the basketball team received a twenty-five dollar prize.

University of Kentucky. The athletic teams at the University of Kentucky in Lexington were nicknamed the *Wildcats* in 1909 when it was said that "the Kentucky football team fought like wildcats" in reference to its victory over the University of Illinois.

Kenyon College. Kenyon College's athletic teams are nicknamed the *Lords* because two English noblemen, Lord Kenyon and Lord Gambier, provided most of the money used to establish this Ohio college in 1824. The town in which Kenyon sits is named Gambier.

Lehigh University. Athletes at Lehigh University in Bethlehem, Pennsylvania, are nicknamed the *Engineers* due to the university's early reputation for excellence in engineering.

University of Louisville. The athletic teams at the University of Louisville have been nicknamed the *Cardinals* since the early part of the century. This name was chosen because the cardinal is the state bird of Kentucky.

Lynchburg College. Lynchburg College's athletic teams were nicknamed the *Hornets* because a small lake on the 214-acre campus in Virginia is a popular breeding ground for hornets.

University of Maine. The University of Maine athletic teams were nicknamed the *Black Bears* in 1913 when two black bear cubs regularly appeared at the football games.

University of Maryland. The athletic teams at the University of Maryland are called the *Terrapins*. It was university President H. C. Byrd, who recommended the nickname *Diamondbacks* after the diamondback terrapin (a turtle that predominated in the state). Instead the nickname *Terrapins* was adopted.

163

Massachusetts Institute of Technology (MIT). Athletes at MIT in Cambridge are nicknamed the *Engineers* since most graduates receive engineering degrees.

University of Massachusetts at Amherst. The University of Massachusetts nicknamed its teams the *Minutemen* and *Minutewomen* in 1972 by a student vote that replaced the nickname *Redmen*. They decided on *Minutemen* to honor the Massachusetts farmers who were ready to fight at the 1775 battles at Lexington and Concord in a minute's time.

University of Massachusetts at Boston. The athletic teams at the University of Massachusetts were nicknamed the *Beacons* because of the university's proximity to the ship beacons on Boston Harbor and to Beacon Hill.

Miami University. Miami University's teams are nicknamed the *Redskins* after the Miami Indians who once lived in southwestern Ohio, where the university is located.

University of Miami. The University of Miami athletic teams are nicknamed the *Hurricanes* for the stormy weather that seasonally takes it toll on the Florida coast.

Michigan State University. The athletic teams at Michigan State University in Lansing were nicknamed the *Spartans* in 1925 by *Lansing State Journal* sports editor George Alderton. The soldiers from Sparta, the ancient Greek city, were known for their discipline and fierce fighting.

University of Michigan. The University of Michigan's athletic teams in Ann Arbor are known as the *Wolverines* because the state's official animal is the native wolverine.

164

University of Minnesota. The University of Minnesota's teams in Minneapolis are known as the *Gophers* since Minnesota is the "Gopher State."

Mississippi State University. The athletic teams at Mississippi State University in the city also named Mississippi State were nicknamed the *Bulldogs* in 1906 following a football game against Alabama. A writer for the *Memphis Commercial-Appeal* wrote: "The Maroon defense fought with the tenacity of a bulldog." Teams were formerly known as the *Maroons*, in reference to the school's colors, maroon and white.

University of Mississippi. Students at the University of Mississippi in the city of University chose the team nickname the *Rebels* in 1936 after a contest sponsored by the student newspaper, the *Mississippian.* Mississippi of course, fought on the Confederate side during the Civil War.

University of Missouri at Kansas City. The University of Missouri adopted the nickname the *Kangaroos* for its athletes in 1933 because kangaroo rhymes with KCU and at the time, two baby kangaroos had been recently acquired by the city's Swope Park Zoo.

University of Missouri at St. Louis. Teams at the University of Missouri were nicknamed the *Rivermen* a year after the school was founded. The students selected the nickname because no other school had the name and because St. Louis is located on the Mississippi and Missouri rivers.

Montana State University. Athletic teams at Montana State University were nicknamed the *Bobcats* in 1916 by Lester Cole, the editor of the *Montana Exponent*, and Fred Bullock, the sports editor. Cole wrote: "The name *Bobcat* was selected first because the name was that of an animal who is

165

crafty, a fighter, not large but respected; one that is wild, uses teamwork of claws and teeth, and mixes cunning with brute strength in every battle."

University of Montana. The University of Montana in Missoula nicknamed its teams the *Grizzlies* after the grizzly, or brown bear, which is native to the state.

University of Nebraska at Lincoln. Teams at the University of Nebraska were nicknamed the *Cornhuskers* in 1900 by Charles S. "Cy" Sherman, the sports editor of the *Lincoln Star*. He coined the nickname in reference to Nebraska, a prominent corn-growing state.

University of Nebraska at Omaha. Teams at the University of Nebraska were nicknamed the *Mavericks* following a student vote in 1972. They were originally the *Cardinals*, from 1913 until 1947, then switched to the *Indians* to avoid confusion with the local professional baseball team.

University of Nevada at Las Vegas. The athletic teams at the University of Nevada received the nickname the *Rebels* in 1958 when the official name of the school at that time was Nevada Southern University. They received this nickname because Nevada became a state in 1864 (during the Civil War).

University of Nevada at Reno. The University of Nevada's athletic teams were originally nicknamed the *Wolves* in 1921, but they gradually became known as the *Wolf Pack*, a reference to the teamwork nature of a wolf pack.

University of New Hampshire. The University of New Hampshire adopted the nickname the *Wildcats* for its teams in 1926 in honor of the school's mascot, a wildcat that was captured by a farmer in Meredith, New Hampshire.

New Mexico State University. The men's athletic teams at New Mexico State University in Las Cruces are nicknamed the *Aggies* because agriculture is a major area of study there. The women's teams are called the *Roadrunners*, since the bird is indigenous to the area.

University of New Mexico. Teams at the University of New Mexico in Albuquerque were nicknamed the *Lobos* after a government trapper caught a wolf pup in Western New Mexico in 1926 and donated it to the university as a mascot. *Lobo* is a Spanish word that means "wolf."

University of New Orleans. The University of New Orleans athletic teams were nicknamed the *Privateers* by the students because a few centuries ago a group of privateers, or pirates, who were commissioned by the U.S. government to destroy the ships of enemy countries gathered at the port of New Orleans.

New York University. The athletic teams at New York University in New York City were nicknamed the *Violets* because the university surrounds Washington Square Park, where many violets grew.

North Carolina State University. Raleigh's North Carolina State University's football team was nicknamed the *Wolfpack* in 1922 after a fan, upset with the poor season, complained to athletic officials that the team could never have a winning record as long as they acted like a wolfpack on and off the field. Despite many objections, students started calling the football team the *Wolfpack*, which in 1947 came to be the nickname for all of the school's varsity teams.

University of North Carolina at Chapel Hill. The athletic teams at the University of North Carolina are nicknamed the *Tar Heels* because North Carolina is the *Tar Heel State.*

North Dakota State University. North Dakota State University's athletic teams were nicknamed the *Bisons* in 1919 by the head football coach Stan Borleske in honor of the huge herds of North American bison that once roamed the plains of North Dakota.

University of North Dakota. The University of North Dakota athletic teams were nicknamed the *Fighting Sioux* after the Sioux Indians of the Great Plains. The University graduates many American Indians.

Northeastern University. The athletic teams at Northeastern University in Boston were nicknamed the *Huskies* in 1927 after their new mascot, which was imported from Alaska.

Northwestern University. Northwestern University's athletic teams in Evanston, Illinois, were nicknamed the *Wildcats* in 1924 by a *Chicago Tribune* sports writer who wrote, "Football players had not come down from Evanston; Wildcats would be a better name . . . ," after Northwestern's football team performed courageously against Chicago and Notre Dame.

Notre Dame University. The athletic teams at Notre Dame University in South Bend, Indiana, are known as the *Fighting Irish* because of the Catholic school's Irish heritage. This is the most famous nickname of all U.S. colleges.

Ohio State University. Ohio State University's athletic teams are called the *Buckeyes* after the state's nickname. The nickname comes from the buckeye trees that flourish in Ohio.

Ohio University. In 1925 Ohio University's athletic board in Athens sponsored a contest to find a nickname and mascot for the athletic teams. Alumnus Hal H. Rowland took home the ten-dollar prize for submitting the *Bobcats*, which was chosen to exemplify the school's fighting spirit.

Oklahoma State University. Oklahoma State University's athletic teams were nicknamed the *Cowboys* and *Cowgirls* in 19w0 because of the huge agricultural department at the school in Stillwater. The school was named Oklahoma A&M College until 1957.

University of Oklahoma. The University of Oklahoma athletic teams in Norman were nicknamed the *Sooners* in 1908 after the state's nickname, the *Sooner State*. Like the "sooners" of the 1890s, the school's athletes, run ahead of their competition.

Oregon State University. Corvallis's Oregon State University's athletic teams are nicknamed the *Beavers* because Oregon is known as the *Beaver State*. Beavers proliferated throughout the state in earlier times; also, the beaver is associated with intelligence, industry, and ingenuity.

University of Oregon. The athletic teams at the University of Oregon in Eugene are nicknamed the *Ducks*. They were originally called the *Webfooters* by the local media in the 1920s, but became the *Ducks* in the 1930s.

Penn State University. The athletic teams at Penn State University were nicknamed the *Nittany Lions* in 1906 because the college lies in the Nittany Valley at the foot of Mount Nittany and mountain lions are said to have once roamed the mountains in central Pennsylvania.

University of Pennsylvania. The athletic teams at the University of Pennsylvania in Philadelphia were nicknamed the *Quakers* because Pennsylvania was once owned by William Penn, who was a Quaker and encouraged Quaker settlement. School officials prefer calling them the *Red and Blue,* since these are the team's colors.

Pepperdine University. Even though Pepperdine University now sits on the Pacific Ocean in Malibu, California, the athletic teams were named the *Waves* in 1937 when the campus was located in downtown Los Angeles. College president Dr. Batsell Barrett Baxter had frequently talked of the "great blue waters of the Pacific" in his speeches and students picked up on his remarks and chose the nickname the *Waves.*

University of Pittsburgh at Pittsburgh. The University of Pittsburgh's athletic teams were nicknamed the *Panthers* in 1909 at a meeting of students and alumni leaders. According to student George M. P. Baird, he selected the panther because it was a formidable creature once indigenous to the area; it had ancient, heraldic standing as a noble animal; it was a perfect alliteration; it was close in color to one of the university's colors, old gold; and because no other college at the time had a panther as its mascot.

Portland State University. Portland State University in Oregon nicknamed its teams the *Vikings* in 1947 when the school was still Vanport College. Vanport chose the nickname because of its location on the Columbia River, where Vikings were associated with fighters and warriors, and because the nickname fit nicely with the college.

University of Portland. The athletic teams at the University of Portland in Oregon were named the *Pilots* in reference to the city's location as a major Pacific port and the ship's pilots who maneuver the ships in and out of the port.

Princeton University. The athletic teams at Princeton in New Jersey were nicknamed the *Tigers* in 1880 by the local

since the 1930s when the school was known as Texas School of Mines.

University of Texas at San Antonio. The sports teams at the University of Texas at San Antonio were nicknamed the *Roadrunners* in 1977 through a university-wide selection. The name was chosen because the bird is speedy and native to the Southwest.

Tufts University. Athletic teams at Tufts University in Medford, Massachusetts, were nicknamed the *Jumbos* after Jumbo the elephant, which had been given to the school by Phineas T. Barnum, the famous circus owner and a trustee at the university.

Tulane University. New Orleans's Tulane University's athletic teams were nicknamed the *Green Wave* in 1920 by Earl Sparling, editor of the student paper *Hullabaloo*. The name came from a football song that he wrote titled, "The Rolling Green Wave."

University of Tulsa. Oklahoma's University of Tulsa's athletic teams were first nicknamed the *Golden Tornadoes* in 1922 by the head football coach, who commented that his team roared through their opponents "like tornadoes." It was soon discovered that Georgia Tech had the same nickname, so the school changed the name to the *Golden Hurricane*.

U.S. Coast Guard Academy. Located in New London, Connecticut, the athletic teams at the U.S. Coast Guard Academy are nicknamed the *Bears* after Objee, their bear mascot.

U.S. Military Academy. The U.S. Military Academy's sport teams at West Point are nicknamed the *Black Knights* because black is one of their team colors and because of their fighting spirit.

U.S. Naval Academy. The U.S. Naval Academy's athletic teams at Annapolis are called the *Midshipmen.* Midshipmen are students who train at any college for the navy.

Utah State University. Utah State University's athletic teams are nicknamed the *Aggies* because in its earlier years, the school was called Utah State Agricultural College.

University of Utah. The athletic teams at the University of Utah are nicknamed the *Utes* and the *Lady Utes* after the Ute tribe that is native to the region.

Vanderbilt University. The athletic teams at Vanderbilt University in Nashville were nicknamed the *Commodores* and *Lady Commodores* in 1897 by William E. Beard, a member of the editorial staff of the *Nashville Banner.* He named the teams for Commodore Cornelius Vanderbilt, who funded the grant for the school.

Vassar College. Vassar College's athletic teams are nicknamed the *Brewers* because the founder of the school, Matthew Vassar, was a well-known brewer of beer in the area of Poughkeepsie, New York.

University of Vermont. The athletic teams at the University of Vermont were nicknamed the *Catamounts* in the 1940s by the students because the catamount, a member of the mountain lion family, is native to the region.

Villanova University. Athletic teams at Villanova University in Villanova, Pennsylvania, were nicknamed the *Wildcats* by the students in 1926 because they have the fighting spirit and the skills of a wildcat.

University of Virginia. The athletic teams at the University of Virginia in Charlottesville are nicknamed the *Cavaliers* after "The Cavalier Song," written by Lawrence Lee, Jr.

Wake Forest University. The athletic teams at Wake Forest University in North Carolina were nicknamed the *Demon Deacons* by Mayon Parker, editor of the school paper, after a devilish win over Trinity (which is now Duke University).

Washington State University. The athletic teams at Washington State University were nicknamed the *Cougars* in 1919 by an Oakland, California, cartoonist after the team defeated Berkeley 14-0 in football.

University of Washington. The University of Washington's athletic teams were nicknamed the *Huskies* in 1921 because the name represented the true spirit of the growing Northwest as the gateway to Alaska. A husky is an Eskimo-bred dog that is strong and trained to pull dog sleds.

West Virginia University. The athletic teams at West Virginia University are nicknamed the *Mountaineers* for the tradition of freedom and rugged individual spirit in the state.

Wichita State University. The sport teams at Wichita State University in Kansas were nicknamed the *Shuckers* in 1905 because the football players shucked corn during the summer for extra money.

University of Wisconsin at Madison. The athletic teams at the University of Wisconsin were nicknamed the *Badgers* after the state's nickname, the *Badger State*.

University of Wyoming. The University of Wyoming athletic teams are called the *Cowboys* and *Cowgirls* after the spirit of the old western college that was established in Laramie in 1886.

Yale University. The athletic teams at Yale University in New Haven are called the *Bulldogs* and *Elis*. They are called the *Bulldogs* because of their persistent fighting nature and *Elis* in honor of Elihu Yale, after whom the university was named.

The Ivy League. It is commonly thought that this term is a reference to the ivy-covered walls associated with the old northeastern colleges. But the term actually goes back to the "Four League" of the mid-nineteenth century, an interscholastic league formed by Harvard, Yale, Princeton, and Columbia. The name of the league was always written in proper academic fashion in Roman numerals—IV League—and commonly pronounced as the "Ivy League." The term came into general use in the 1930s after sportswriter Caswell Adams used it to refer to Princeton and Columbia. It wasn't until after World War II, however, that the ten northeastern schools formed what we now know as the Ivy League.

THE NAME OF THE GAME IS SPORTS

■

Some of the most colorful nicknames in America are the ones you'll hear in the realm of sports. In fact, an athlete of almost any importance will be tagged with one. After all, every team gets a nickname, so why shouldn't its members? This chapter focuses on, but isn't limited to, nicknames in the major U.S. sports.

MAJOR LEAGUE BASEBALL

Have you ever wondered how major league baseball teams got their names? Most people cheer for their favorite teams not even knowing why they're called what they are. Some teams even have nicknames. It seems to be just part of the game.

Atlanta Braves. The Braves were named after James E. Gaffney, the owner of the ball club and a political "brave" from New York's Tammany Hall in 1911 when the team was located in Boston. The Braves have kept the name ever since except from 1935–1940 when they were called the *Boston Bees.* In 1952 the team moved to Milwaukee where they were known as the Milwaukee Braves until they moved to Atlanta in 1966.

179

Baltimore Orioles. The Baltimore Orioles were originally called the Lord Baltimores in 1901 after George Calvert, the first Lord Baltimore who governed the British colony of Maryland in 1632. They were later called the Baltimore Orioles in honor of Maryland's official state bird.

Boston Red Sox. The Red Sox became the official nickname of Boston's baseball team in 1907 because team owner John Irvin Taylor's son liked the color of the stockings the players were wearing.

California Angels. Gene Autry, the founder of the California Angels, named the team in 1961 because the team was based in Los Angeles, which is known as the "City of Angels." The team later moved to Anaheim but kept the name.

Chicago Cubs. The Chicago Cubs were officially named in 1907. Years earlier, a newspaper writer had used *Cubs* as a nickname because it was a short name to fit headlines.

Chicago White Sox. Chicago's baseball team was originally called the White Stockings when founded in 1900, but two years later, sportswriters Sy Sanborn and Earl Green shortened the name to the Chicago White Sox to better fit headlines.

Cincinnati Reds. The Cincinnati Reds baseball team was originally called the "Red Stockings" for its colorful uniforms when founded in 1869. It was later shortened to the Reds in the 1890s. Due to the communist scare in the 1950s, the name was briefly changed to the *Redlegs*, because the "Reds" was thought by some to be synonymous with "communists."

Cleveland Indians. Cleveland's baseball team was named the Indians in 1913 in honor of former Cleveland player

Luis Francis Sockalexis, also known as "Chief," the first American Indian to play in the major leagues.

Detroit Tigers. Detroit's baseball team was named the Tigers by George Stallings, manager for the Detroit baseball team in 1896, because he dressed the players in black and brown stockings, which reminded him of tigers.

Houston Astros. Houston's major league baseball team was originally called the Houston Colt 45's after Judge Roy Hofheinz fired the Colt 45 into the ground at the opening ceremony of the new multi-sports facility in 1961. The Colt 45 was chosen because it was the pistol that won the West. In April 1965, the team was renamed the Astros with the completion of the Houston Astrodome.

Kansas City Royals. Kansas City's baseball team was named the Royals by its fans during its first year in 1968. A contest held to pick a name netted 17,000 suggestions. The winner won an all-expense paid trip to the major league All-Star game at the Houston Astrodome.

Los Angeles Dodgers. The Los Angeles Dodgers inherited the name *Dodgers* from their days in Brooklyn, New York. Brooklyn's baseball team was organized in 1890 as the "Brooklyn Trolley Dodgers" because of the numerous streetcars in the borough. In those days, people had to dodge streetcars when walking in Brooklyn. The name was later shortened to the "Dodgers"; from 1899–1905 the name was "Superbas"; from 1914–1931 the team was known as the "Robins." Then it was back to the Dodgers and even after the team headed to Los Angeles in 1958, the name remained the same. In the east, they were frequently referred to as the Brooklyn Bums, but that name was left behind after the move to the West Coast.

181

Milwaukee Brewers. The Milwaukee Brewers were named in 1970 after the bankrupt Seattle Pilots moved their franchise to Wisconsin. They were named the *Brewers* because Milwaukee is called "the beer capitol of the world."

Minnesota Twins. The Minnesota Twins were originally named the "Twin Cities Twins" after the Washington Senators moved to Minnesota in 1960. The team name was inspired by the twin cities of Minneapolis and St. Paul, which are separated by the Mississippi River. Calvin Griffith, the team president, decided to change the name to the Minnesota Twins before the first season.

Montreal Expos. The Montreal Expos were founded and named in 1967 in honor of the world's fair, often referred to as Expo '67, which was held in Montreal Canada.

New York Mets. The New York Mets were named in 1961 by club owner Joan Payson. The name is a derivative of the team's corporate name, Metropolitan Baseball Club. It was also descriptive of New York's metropolitan area, and the sportswriters loved it for its brevity.

New York Yankees. The New York Yankees were named in 1909 for the era's rising nationalism, when the term *Yankee* was used as a synonym for "American."

Oakland Athletics. The Athletics team originated in Philadelphia in 1900. Its name comes from the Athletics Men's Club. After 55 seasons, the team moved to Kansas City. In 1968, the team moved to Oakland, where it is more popularly called the Oakland A's.

Philadelphia Phillies. The Philadelphia Phillies were nicknamed in 1883 because the city of Philadelphia is often referred to as "Philly."

Pittsburgh Pirates. Pittsburgh's baseball team was originally called the Pittsburgh Alleghenies when it was founded in 1876. The name was in honor of the region's Allegheny River and the Allegheny Mountains (Pittsburgh is also in Allegheny County). In the 1890s, the nickname was changed to the Pirates because the team illegally "pirated" player Louis Bierbauer from Philadelphia's team.

San Diego Padres. The San Diego Padres were named for the Spanish *padres* ("fathers," priests) who were honored for building a chain of missions throughout California during the eighteenth and nineteenth centuries. Located at the Mexican border, the city has a strong Spanish influence.

San Francisco Giants. The San Francisco Giants were named when the team was located in New York City. After a big win in 1886, team manager Jim Mutrie proclaimed to his team, originally known as the Gothams, "My big fellows! My giants! We are the people!" From then on, the team has been known as the Giants. They moved to San Francisco in 1957.

Seattle Mariners. Seattle's baseball team was named the Mariners on August 24, 1976, after club officials held a contest to choose a name for the new team. The name was chosen because of the natural association between the sea and Seattle and its people.

St. Louis Cardinals. The St. Louis Cardinals were named around the turn of the century when their brown uniforms were changed to include a bright red trim. Willie McHale, a sportswriter for the *St. Louis Republic*, referred to the team as the St. Louis Cardinals after overhearing a woman who saw the new uniforms comment, "What a lovely shade of cardinal."

Texas Rangers. After the Washington Senators moved to Dallas-Fort Worth, Texas, in 1971, a public contest was held to name the new team. Texas Rangers was the winner, an obvious reference to the famed mounted police force of the 1800s.

Toronto Blue Jays. The Toronto Blue Jays were named following a contest in 1976. The name Blue Jays was selected because of the vast amount of these birds in the area surrounding Toronto.

The Greatest Baseball Players' Nicknames

Willie (Ack Ack) Aikens. "Ack Ack" is a reference to Aikens being a stutterer.

George (Sparky) Anderson. "Sparky" because a sportswriter in Fort Worth wrote about sparks flying when Anderson argued with umpires.

Walter (Boom Boom) Beck. "Boom Boom" because of this pitcher's lack of expertise. "The first boom was the ball hitting the bat, and the second boom was the ball hitting the outfield wall," writes Peter Golenbock in *Bums.*

Lawrence (Yogi) Berra. "Yogi" by his teenage friends because he resembled an actor called Yogi in a movie.

Tom (The Flamingo) Brennan. "The Flamingo" because when he pitched, he kicked his left knee waist-high and held it there while he perched on his right leg.

Roger (The Rocket) Clemens. "The Rocket" because he is a fastball strikeout pitcher for the Boston Red Sox.

184

Ty (The Georgia Peach) Cobb. "Georgia Peach" because he was a native of Georgia.

Bill (Doggie) Dawley. "Doggie" because he wore a Pluto hat that he had bought at Disney World during spring training.

The Diaper Squad. The 1960 Orioles's pitching rotation was called the *Diaper Squad* because every member (Chuck Estrada, Jack Fisher, Milt Pappas, Jerry Walker, and Steve Barber) was under 23 years old.

(Joltin') Joe DiMaggio. "Joltin' Joe" by sportswriters after he led the league with a .381 average during the 1939 season.

Walt (Moose) Dropo. "Moose" because he once lived in Moosup, Connecticut.

Leo (The Lip) Durocher. "The Lip" because of his talkative nature as an infielder and manager.

Mark (The Bird) Fidrych. "The Bird" because of his frizzy hair, long legs, and lopsided stride. Fidrych would also let out a high-pitched sound when excited, much resembling a bird.

Carlton (Pudge) Fisk. "Pudge" when he was in eighth grade because he was 5 feet, 4 inches and weighed 155 pounds.

Lou (The Iron Horse) Gehrig. "Iron Horse" because he was as durable as a horse during his 2,130-game career.

Richard Michael (The Exorcist) Gossage. "The Exorcist" because when he stood on the mound he scared the hell out of you.

Harvey (The Kitten) Haddix. "The Kitten" because of his resemblance to Harry "The Cat" Breechen.

James (Catfish) Hunter. "Catfish" because he was from North Carolina and had done a lot of fishing.

(Shoeless) Joe Jackson. "Shoeless" because he played baseball shoeless in the park.

Reggie (Mr. October) Jackson. "Mr. October" by Yankee teammate Thurman Munson for his key hitting during his 1977 league championship series. Jackson hit 563 home runs during his career, but his 16 in postseason play during the month of October helped earn him his nickname.

Tommy (The Godfather) Lasorda. "The Godfather" because he once put a head of a pig with an apple in its mouth in Los Angeles Dodgers Steve Sax's bed, with a note that read: "Play better baseball—or else." It was signed "The Godfather."

Jeff (Penitentiary Face) Leonard. "Penitentiary Face" because of his mean looks and fighting nature.

Albert (Sparky) Lyle. According to Albert, he got nicknamed because "my parents thought they were gonna have a dog."

Mickey (The Commerce Comet) Mantle. "The Commerce Comet" because he was from Commerce, Oklahoma, and hit some long home runs during the 1950 season that fans called "comets."

Christy (Big Six) Mathewson. "Big Six" after the New York City Fire Department's fastest engine. This was fitting due to his legendary fastball with the New York Giants that earned him induction into the Baseball Hall of Fame.

Willie (The Say-Hey Kid) Mays. "The Say-Hey Kid" when he first came to the New York Giants. He didn't know anybody's name so he'd shout, "Say hey, over there!"

John (The Count) Montefusco. "The Count" because his name rhymed with the title character of Alexandre Dumas's novel *The Count of Monte Cristo.*

Phil (Father Time) Niekro. "Father Time" because he was the oldest player in the majors.

Jim (Cakes) Palmer. "Cakes" after he attributed a shutout game to the pancakes he had for breakfast when he was 19 years old.

Dave (The Cobra) Parker. "The Cobra" because of his venomous strikes at opposing pitchers.

Jeff (The Terminator) Reardon. "The Terminator" because once he got released from the bullpen the game would be over!

Harold (Pee Wee) Reese. "Pee Wee" because, according to Reese, "I was the marbles champion of Louisville, and Pee Wee was my shooter. I didn't use an immie. I used a pee wee." (For all you non-marble shooters, a shooter, an immie and a pee wee are names for certain marbles.)

John Milton (Gozzlehead) Rivers. "Gozzlehead" because that was what he called everyone else.

Pete (Charlie Hustle) Rose. "Charlie Hustle" during spring training of 1963 when Pete was only 21 years old. Pitcher Whitey Ford gave him this nickname because of his speed to first base.

George Herman (Babe) Ruth. According to Ruth, he got the nickname when scout Jack Dunn brought him to the Orioles clubhouse for the first time and Sam Steinman said, "Here comes Dunnie with his newest babe."

Nolan (The Ryan Express) Ryan. "The Ryan Express" was given to Nolan by the media in reference to a 1965 movie *Von Ryan's Express.* They were comparing his pitching speed with that of a speeding train.

Mike (Titlest Head) Schmidt. "Titlest Head" because his skin troubles reminded his Phillies teammates of the surface of a golf ball.

Tom (Terrific) Seaver. "Terrific" because of his outstanding career.

Mike (Sony) Stenhouse. "Sony" is a result of a string of bases on balls he received as a pinch hitter. The nickname refers to the makers of the Walkman.

Frank (The Pittsburgh Stealer) Tavares. "The Pittsburgh Stealer" because he stole more than 200 bases for the Pirates.

The Mookie Ball

In 1992, actor Charlie Sheen paid $93,500 for the baseball that slipped between Bill Buckner's legs and ultimately cost the Boston Red Sox the 1986 World Series. The ball is named after Mookie Wilson, the New York Mets player who hit the ball past Buckner at first base.

Ted (The Splendid Splinter) Williams. "The Splendid Splinter" refers to his batting stance and slim body as a young player.

Willie (Mookie) Wilson. "Mookie" when he was growing up in South Carolina. This is how he pronounced *milk* as a baby and the name stayed with him.

BASEBALL'S TOP 20 NICKNAMES

1. Lefty	11. Tex
2. Red	12. Pop
3. Doc	13. Babe
4. Bud/Buddy	14. Chief
5. Dutch	15. Heinie
6. Big (Jim, Bill, etc.)	16. Pete
7. Mickey	17. Fritz
8. Whitey	18. Cy
9. Chick	19. Moose
10. Kid	20. Deacon

FOOTBALL TEAM NAMES

Atlanta Falcons. The Atlanta Falcons were named in 1965 following a contest held by team officials and a radio station. The winner's submission of the Falcons was chosen because the falcon is proud and dignified, with great courage and flight. It never drops its prey.

Buffalo Bills. The Buffalo Bills were named in 1946 by a contest. The name was chosen for Buffalo Bill Cody, the famous hero of the West, and because owner Jim Breuil's company (Frontier Oil) opened a new frontier in sports in western New York.

Chicago Bears. The Chicago Bears were named in the 1920s by founder George Halas because they were known as the "Monsters of the Midway" and had a reputation for being fierce and nasty.

Cincinnati Bengals. The Cincinnati Bengals were named after a former pro football team named the Bengals that played from 1937–1941. Paul Brown, the Bengals coach and general manager stated, "In naming them Bengals, we mean tigers, not the lancers."

Cleveland Browns. In 1945 team officials ran a contest to name the Cleveland football team. The *Panthers* was chosen, but unfortunately, there was a semi-pro football team near Cleveland already named the Panthers; even worse, they were chronic losers. Following another contest, many entries suggested the "Brown Bombers," either because of the team colors or because of the team's coach and general manger, Paul Brown, who shortened the name to the Browns.

Dallas Cowboys. The Dallas Cowboys were originally named the Dallas Rangers in reference to the police force that once roamed the Lone Star State (the Texas Rangers). The team changed its name to the Dallas Cowboys shortly after-

ward because there was already a local minor league baseball team called the Rangers.

Denver Broncos. The Denver Broncos were named via a
contest conducted in 1959, following their acceptance into
the league. The name had been used by a baseball team,
in Denver in the 1920s. It symbolized the toughness and
determination of the west.

Detroit Lions. The Detroit Lions were named in 1934 partly
because of the success the Detroit Tigers baseball team was
having and because "the lion is monarch of the jungle,"
according to Cy Houston, vice-president and general manager of the team.

Green Bay Packers. The Green Bay Packers were named
after the corporation that paid to start the team in 1919.
Curly Lambeau, who came up with the idea to form the
team, worked at the Indian Packing Company in Green
Bay. He got the company to sponsor the team, and to provide equipment and a practice field.

Houston Oilers. The Houston Oilers were founded and
named by K. S. "Bud" Adams in 1959. He named the team
in honor of the industry that enabled him to purchase
the team.

Indianapolis Colts. The Indianapolis Colts were known as
the Baltimore Colts until 1984. The Baltimore team was
named through a contest in 1946, when the bankrupt
Miami Seahawks moved there.

Kansas City Chiefs. The Kansas City Chiefs were named
through a contest in 1963 after the Dallas Texans football
team moved to Kansas City.

191

Los Angeles Raiders. The Los Angeles Raiders were named by team officials when they were located in Oakland. Their previous name, the Metropolitan Oakland Area Football Club, was considered too long for public use and especially for headlines when founded in 1960. The Oakland team moved to Los Angeles in 1982 and kept the name.

Los Angeles Rams. The Los Angeles Rams were named in 1937 when they were still located in Cleveland. Founder Homer Marshman and general manager Buzz Wetzel were on the lookout for a new name. "If there is one college team that has a name I really like, it's the Fordham Rams," Wetzel said. After hearing the suggestion, Marshman agreed.

Miami Dolphins. The Miami Dolphins were named by a contest in 1965. "The dolphin is one of the fastest and smartest creatures of the sea," according to team owner Joseph Robbie in explaining why they picked the name. "Dolphins can attack and kill a shark or a whale. Sailors say bad luck will come to anyone who harms one of them."

Minnesota Vikings. The Minnesota Vikings were nicknamed by General Manager Bert Rose in 1961. He picked the name because the Nordic Vikings were known for their fearlessness, aggressiveness, and desire to win. Minnesota is also an area rich in Nordic background.

New England Patriots. The New England Patriots got their name in 1960 when a contest was held to name the new football team. The Boston Patriots was selected in honor of the eighteenth-century colonists who helped declare independence from Britain. The name was changed to the New England Patriots after the team moved outside of the Boston vicinity in 1970.

New Orleans Saints. The New Orleans Saints were named in 1967 because the franchise was awarded to the city on All Saints Day in 1966. Some believe the team was named after the famous jazz song, "When the Saints Come Marching In," in reference to the city's love for jazz.

New York Giants. The New York Giants were named in 1925 after New York's baseball team the New York Giants.

New York Jets. The New York Jets (formerly the New York Titans) were named in 1963 because the country was entering the "jet age" or "space age" and because the team's new field, Shea Stadium, was going to be located between New York's two main airports, La Guardia and Idlewild (now John F. Kennedy).

Philadelphia Eagles. The Philadelphia Eagles were named during the Great Depression of the 1930s in honor of President Franklin Roosevelt's New Deal and National Recovery Act. It was a patriotic gesture for the city of Brotherly Love to name its football team in honor of the bald eagle.

Phoenix Cardinals. The Phoenix Cardinals were named in 1898 when they were founded in Chicago. They were named for the color of their uniforms, which was cardinal red. Although they moved to St. Louis, Missouri, in 1960 and then to Phoenix, Arizona, in 1988, the name has never changed.

Pittsburgh Steelers. The Pittsburgh Steelers were named in 1940 by the team founder Art Rooney. They were originally called the Pittsburgh Pirates when founded in 1933 after the city's baseball team, but switched to properly represent the city known as the "Steel Capitol of the World."

San Diego Chargers. The San Diego Chargers were named by a contest in 1959 when the team was located in Los Angeles. Although the team moved to San Diego in 1961, they kept the name.

San Francisco 49ers. The San Francisco 49ers were named in the late 1940s by part-owner Alan Sorrell to honor the 1849 California Gold Rush. Since there were very few pro football teams west of the Mississippi River, Sorrell felt team owners were taking a risk establishing a team in San Francisco, just as the gold prospectors, also called 49ers, took a risk in 1849.

Seattle Seahawks. The Seattle Seahawks were named in 1975, a year after being founded. The name was chosen by a "name the team" contest. According to team general manager John Thompson, "Our new name shows aggressiveness, reflects our soaring Northwest heritage, and belongs to no other major league team."

Tampa Bay Buccaneers. The Tampa Bay Buccaneers were named by a radio station contest in 1975. The winning name was chosen based on the pirates who sailed Florida's coastal waters.

Washington Redskins. The Washington Redskins were named in 1933 when the team was located in Boston. They were originally called the Duluth Eskimos in the late 1920s and early 1930s. When they moved to Boston in 1932, they became the Boston Braves, since they played in the Braves' baseball stadium. In 1933, the team moved to Fenway Park, the Boston Red Sox stadium, and switched their name to the Redskins to honor the Red Sox. In 1937, the team moved to Washington, D.C., and the name stayed the same.

194

Football Players' Nicknames

Eric (The Flea) Allen. "The Flea" because he always dogged defenders.

(Slingin') Sammy Baugh. "Slingin' " because of his accuracy as a quarterback.

Robert (Rocky) Bleier. Shortly after being born, his father declared, "The son of a bitch looks like a little rock."

Robert (Dr. Doom) Brazile. "Dr. Doom" when he was the only college all-star game linebacker in 1975 without a nickname. "We had 'Spiderman' and 'Batman'," recalled Brazile. "They took my name right out of the comics, right out of the *Chicago Tribune.*"

Paul (Bear) Bryant. "Bear" was a name given to Alabama's immortal coach because he once wrestled a bear at a carnival.

Glen (Mr. Outside) Davis. "Mr. Outside" because he was the end-around running mate of Doc "Mr. Inside" Blanchard when he played at West Point.

Eric (Mr. Benny) Dickerson. "Mr. Benny" because he was known to be very cheap (a reference to the late comedian Jack Benny, who played up his reputation as a skinflint).

(Iron Mike) Ditka. "Iron Mike" because he was an endurance player.

Brent (Allstate) Duhon. "Allstate" because he was the team's insurance against dropped balls as a wide receiver at Texas.

195

Red (The Galloping Ghost) Grange. "The Galloping Ghost" was a suitable nickname for this immortal speed demon. Sportswriter Grantland Rice coined it.

(Mean) Joe Greene. "Mean Joe" was a reference to Greene's aggressive nature as a Pittsburgh Steelers defensive end. His friends say Greene is a sweet, gentle man.

Thomas (Hollywood) Henderson. "Hollywood" because he was always in the spotlight as a Dallas Cowboy. Ironically, it wasn't until after he was nicknamed Hollywood that he appeared in episodes of television series such as "Buck Rogers in the 25th Century" and "B. J. and the Bear."

Craig (Ironhead) Heyward. "Ironhead" because he grew up in Pittsburgh, the "Steel City."

Rod (Shrine Game) Hill. "Shrine Game" became the nickname for this Dallas Cowboy who ran east and west but rarely forward while returning punts. The shrine game is played by the best players from the east against the best players from the west.

Elroy (Crazy Legs) Hirsch. "Crazy Legs" because this L.A. Ram ran like a cartoon character.

Lionel (Little Train) James. "Little Train" because people named "Lionel" are commonly nicknamed "Train," and this one was only 5 feet, 6 inches.

Thomas (Pepper) Johnson. "Pepper" because when he was a kid, he put pepper on his cereal.

Dick (Night Train) Lane. "Night Train" because this Lions Hall of Fame defensive back loved the bandleader's rendition of "Night Train."

Louis (Hot) Lipps. "Hot" after this receiver made a series of surprising catches with the Pittsburgh Steelers—and "Hot" goes well with "Lipps" (of *M*A*S*H* fame).

Howie (Caveman) Long. "Caveman" because Long has Neanderthal looks.

Calvin (CNN) Muhammad. "CNN" because he broadcasts 24 hours a day. His teammates say he never stops talking.

(Broadway) Joe Namath. "Broadway" because he was the star of the New York Jets, and a real showman.

Nate (The Kitchen) Newton. "The Kitchen" because upon arrival at the Cowboy's training camp, he weighed in at 332 pounds.

Walter (Sweetness) Payton. "Sweetness" because he was such a sweet (good) runner.

Elvis (Toast) Patterson. "Toast" because this New York Giant cornerback was always getting burned.

William (The Fridge) Perry. "The Fridge" was a natural for this 330 pounder as a result of all the food he consumed when playing for Clemson University. When he first arrived at the Bears training camp his teammates called him "Biscuit" because they said, "he's just a biscuit away from 350." One of his newer nicknames is "Avalanche" because, according to John Madden, "when he takes off his T-shirt, one happens."

O. J. (The Juice) Simpson. "The Juice" because common belief was that *O. J.* stood for "Orange Juice," not "Orenthal James."

Sylvester (Postage) Stamps. "Postage" because he rarely takes a licking when returning to sender's end zones.

Vinnie (Vincent Priceless) Testaverde. "Vincent Priceless" because this quarterback was invaluable to the University of Miami, where he was a Heisman Trophy winner.

Y. A. (The Bald Eagle) Tittle. "The Bald Eagle" simply because he was bald.

Eddie (Meat Cleaver) Weaver. "Meat Cleaver" because of the way this Georgia defensive lineman hacked up his opponents.

Byron (Whizzer) White. This Yale all-American and Rhodes scholar got nicknamed the "Whizzer" because of the speed with which he gave up his football career for a seat on the U.S. Supreme Court.

More Colorful Football Nicknames

The Crunch Berries. Tony Berry and Dick Berry, two of Kansas's defensive backs, were nicknamed Crunch Berries because they hit so hard.

Doomsday Defense. Pittsburgh's defense has been nicknamed Doomsday Defense because they have twice survived "doomsday"—super bowls 10 and 13.

Fort Landry. The Dallas Cowboys training/boot camp in Thousand Oaks, California, is called Fort Landry because of the strict military regimen coach Tom Landry runs there.

Gerela's Guerillas. Pittsburgh Steeler placekicker Roy Gerela's loyal fans, known as his "foot soldiers," lie down while waiting in the end zone for his kicks.

Ground Chunk. The Seattle Seahawks offense prefers to run the ball on the ground under Coach Chuck Knox.

The Junkyard Dogs. The Chicago Bears defense was called "The Junkyard Dogs," with Bad Leroy Brown, who was supposed to be "meaner than a junkyard dog" (according to the Tom Croce song "Bad Leroy Brown").

The Marino Corps. Dan Marino's loyal fans are known as "The Marino Corps."

The Marks Brothers. Mark Duper and Mark Clayton, two of the Dolphins' wide receivers, are known as "The Marks Brothers."

The New York Sack Exchange. The New York Jets defense has been called "The New York Sack Exchange."

The No-Name Defense. Miami Dolphins defenders were nicknamed "The No-Name Defense" during super bowls 7 and 8 because they were not recognizable stars that the fans knew by name.

The Pittsburgh Maulers. This nickname was coined because Edward DeBartolo, head of the Pittsburgh Steelers, also owns several shopping centers.

BASKETBALL TEAM NAMES

Atlanta Hawks. The Atlanta Hawks were originally the Tri-Cities Blackhawks when founded in 1948. They were named

199

for the famous Sauk Indian Chief Black Hawk. After many moves the team landed in Atlanta, Georgia.

Boston Celtics. The Boston Celtics were named for one of the first truly successful pro basketball teams in the 1920s, the "Original Celtics," founded by Jim Furey. The Boston Celtics were formed in 1946 and the name was chosen by team founder Walter Brown, who stated, "We'll call them the Boston Celtics! The name has a great basketball tradition. And Boston is full of Irishmen. We'll put them in green uniforms and call them the Boston Celtics."

Charlotte Hornets. The Charlotte Hornets were named in 1988 by a contest. The name was chosen in reference to British General Charles Cornwallis, who wrote to the king of England from the Carolinas during the revolutionary war, "This place is like fighting in a hornet's nest."

Chicago Bulls. Richard Klein founded the Chicago Bulls in 1966. He named them the Bulls because the fighting bull, as known from centuries of bull ring history, has a relentless fighting attitude and an instinct never to quit.

Cleveland Cavaliers. The Cleveland Cavaliers were named by a contest when the team was formed. The name *Cavaliers* won because it is good alliteration and means "courteous gentlemen."

Dallas Mavericks. The Mavericks were founded in 1980 and named by a radio contest. The name *Mavericks* won the contest because of the state's identity with the cowboy.

Denver Nuggets. The Denver Nuggets were named after the nineteenth-century rush of people into the area in search of gold and silver. The team was originally called the Denver Rockets when founded in 1967, but the name was changed to the Nuggets in 1974 because another franchise in Houston was already using the name.

Detroit Pistons. The Detroit Pistons originated in 1948 in Fort Wayne, Indiana, as the Fort Wayne Zollner Pistons. Fred Zollner, the team's owner, named them for his company, which had enabled him to purchase the franchise. In 1957, Zollner and the Pistons moved to Detroit, where they fit right in with Detroit's reputation as the "auto capital of the world."

Golden State Warriors. The Golden State Warriors started off as the Philadelphia Warriors in 1946. They were named after the original Philadelphia basketball team, which started playing in the American Basketball League in 1925. In the early 1960s the team moved to San Francisco and were known as the San Francisco Warriors. After moving to Oakland in 1971, they were known as the Golden State Warriors, in an effort to get the whole state of California behind the team.

Houston Rockets. The Houston team was christened the Rockets when it was founded in San Diego in 1967. The name *Rockets* was chosen by a contest because it exemplified the tremendous growth of space-age industries in San Diego. The San Diego Rockets moved to Houston after the 1970–1971 season and became the Houston Rockets. Ironically, this name fits equally as well because the NASA space program is located in Houston.

Indiana Pacers. The Indiana Pacers were named when they were founded in 1967, because they wanted to "set the pace" in professional basketball.

Los Angeles Clippers. The team was named the Buffalo Braves when it moved to San Diego in 1978. The name was changed to better suit San Diego. The Clippers was chosen by a contest in honor of the huge sailing ships, or clippers, that passed through the San Diego harbor many years ago. In 1984, the team moved to Los Angeles but kept the same name.

Los Angeles Lakers. The Los Angeles Lakers were named in 1948 when founded in Minneapolis. They were given this name because Minnesota is known as "The Land of 10,000 Lakes." Although the team moved to Los Angeles, an area with very few lakes, they kept the name.

Miami Heat. The Miami Heat was named in a contest in 1988, the year the team was founded. General partner Zev Bufman said, "The owners just felt it represented the area. When you think of Miami, that's what you think of."

Milwaukee Bucks. The Milwaukee Bucks were named through a contest in 1968, the year the team was founded. Officials picked the entry *Bucks* because it reflects the abundance of wildlife in Wisconsin and, as the winner wrote, "Bucks are spirited, good jumpers, fast, and agile."

Minnesota Timberwolves. The Minnesota Timberwolves were named by a contest in 1989, the year the team was founded. The name was chosen because timber wolves are indigenous to Minnesota (other than Alaska, Minnesota is the only state with a significant number of timber wolves). Also, the name is unique; no other professional sport teams use it.

New Jersey Nets. The New Jersey Nets (formerly the New York Nets) were named in 1968 when they played in New York City. They were named the New York Nets after one of the most important parts of the basketball game: the net. They have since relocated to New Jersey.

New York Knicks. The New York Knicks were named the New York Knickerbockers when founded in 1946. The early Dutch settlers in New York were called Knickerbockers. They wore knickers, which were long trousers banded at the knee.

Orlando Magic. Orlando Magic was named in 1989, the year the team was founded. It was chosen by a contest for the great tourist attractions in the Orlando area (Magic Kingdom and Disney World).

Philadelphia 76ers. The Philadelphia 76ers were named in 1963 in honor of the year the U. S. Declaration of Independence was signed, July 4, 1776, at Philadelphia's Independence Hall. Their team colors are red, white, and blue.

Phoenix Suns. The Phoenix Suns were named in 1968 by a contest to name the team. The name was chosen because of Arizona's year-round sunshine and tropical climate.

Portland Trail Blazers. The Portland Trail Blazers were named in 1970 by a public contest. The team owners stated in a press release: "We feel that Trail Blazers reflects both the ruggedness of the Pacific Northwest and the start of a major league era in our state."

Sacramento Kings. The Sacramento Kings were named when they were founded in Kansas City, Missouri, in 1972. The name was chosen by a contest because team officials wanted it to reflect the standing of the team. When the team moved to Sacramento in 1985, the name moved with them.

San Antonio Spurs. The San Antonio Spurs were named in 1973 by a public contest. The name was picked because it represented the western heritage of Texas.

Seattle Supersonics. The Seattle Supersonics were named by a contest in 1967. At the time, Seattle's Boeing plant was planning on building a Concorde-style airplane known as the "Supersonic Transport." The project never went through, but the Supersonics kept their name.

Utah Jazz. The Utah Jazz was named in 1974 when the team was located in New Orleans. The New Orleans Jazz was named because of the city's reputation as a jazz town. Although Utah is not known for its jazz, the team kept the name when moving to Salt Lake City in 1979.

Washington Bullets. The Washington Bullets were named after the Baltimore Bullets, the original basketball team located in Baltimore in 1946. The Baltimore Bullets were named after a nearby foundry that produced ammunition for U.S. soldiers during World War II but disbanded only a few years later.

Animal Names in Pro Sports

Did you know that nearly 25 percent of the major league professional teams are named for animals? Here's a breakdown:

Animal	Number of Teams
Mammal	13
Bird	9
Fish	2
Insect	1

In case you're wondering, the insect name is the *Charlotte Hornets*.

BASKETBALL'S GREATEST NICKNAMES

Mark (The Pillsbury Doughboy) Aguirre. *The Pillsbury Doughboy* comes from when he weighed 240 pounds in his senior year at DePaul.

Charles (The Round Mound of Rebound) Barkley. *The Round Mound of Rebound* was given to him during his college years at Auburn because he seldom weighed less than 275 pounds.

(Dollar) Bill Bradley. *Dollar Bill* because he was a banker's son and a money player at Princeton and later with the Knicks (before becoming a U.S. senator from New Jersey).

The Bruise Brothers. *The Bruise Brothers* in the early 1980s because the San Antonio Spurs had rough players such as Mark Olberding, Dave Corzine, and Reggie Johnson up front.

Terry (Cadillac) Catledge. *Cadillac,* according to Terry, because, "I'm long, black, and lovely."

Nat (Sweetwater) Clifton. *Sweetwater* because, as one of his girlfriends says, "He was always drinking Pepsi or other kinds of pop. But when that wasn't around, he'd mix sugar with water and drink it."

James (American Tourister) Donaldson. *American Tourister* because "His head's as big as a suitcase," says teammate Darryl Dawkins.

Julius (Dr. J) Erving. *The Doctor* became Erving's nickname in response to his calling his high school teammate, Leon

205

Saunders, *The Professor.* *J* was attached when he joined the ABA by Roland (Fatty) Taylor.

George (The Iceman) Gervin. *The Iceman* because this San Antonio Spurs guard always kept his cool. In his earlier days in Detroit, George walked on his tiptoes, a real cool walk.

Georgi (The Balkan Banger) Glouchkov. *The Balkan Banger* because this Bulgarian lacked finesse on the court.

Darrell (Doctor Dunkenstein) Griffith. *Doctor Dunkenstein* because of his outstanding dunking performances at the University of Louisville.

Earvin (Magic) Johnson. Fred Stabley, Jr., of the *Lansing State Journal,* nicknamed Johnson *Magic* when he was in high school because "Dr. J and the Big E were already taken."

Vinnie (The Microwave) Johnson. *The Microwave* because, "He heats up so fast," according to rival Danny Range.

Spious (Spice) Kilpatrick. *Spice* because that's how they pronounced his first name at New York City's Madison Square Boy's Club many years ago during his youth.

Karl (The Mailman) Malone. *The Mailman* because he always delivers!

(Pistol) Pete Maravich. *Pistol Pete* because of his countless firings at the hoop.

Kevin (The Black Hole) McHale. *The Black Hole* because, according to Celtics teammate Danny Ainge, "When you throw the ball to him, it never comes out."

McHale's Army. While playing for the Boston Celtics, Kevin McHale's loyal fans were called *McHale's Army* after TV's "McHale's Navy."

Reggie (Freddy) Miller. *Freddy* because he wears his hair as closely cropped as Freddy Krueger's, the villain in *Nightmare on Elm Street* movies.

Earl (The Pearl) Monroe. The *Pearl* because he was an invaluable player and because it rhymes with *Earl.*

Tommy (Mascara) Nunez. *Mascara* because this NBA referee is known to lead the league in make-up calls.

Michael (Sugar) Ray Richardson. *Sugar* because his career with the Knicks and Nets was so sweet. Many Rays get tagged with the nickname *Sugar* in honor of the great boxer, Sugar Ray Robinson.

Glenn (Doc) Rivers. *The Doc* because he always wore a Julius (*Dr. J*) Erving shirt at basketball camp in the eighth grade.

Wayne (Tree) Rollins. *Tree* because he stood 7 feet, 1 inch tall and had a head of hair that could have nested a flock of birds.

James (Captain Late) Silas. *Captain Late* because he always seemed to perform at his best during the latter part of games for the San Antonio Spurs.

George (Radar) Stone. *Radar* because of his great range as a forward.

Reece (Goose) Tatum. This ex-Harlem Globetrotter was nicknamed because he had an 84-inch arm span and huge hands.

Andrew (The Boston Strangler) Toney. The *Boston Strangler* in 1982 because of the choke he put on the Boston Celtics during the 1982 Eastern Conference finals.

Melvin (The Great Pumpkin) Turpin. The *Great Pumpkin* because he looked like one in the Cleveland Cavaliers orange uniform.

Anthony (Spud) Webb. *Spud* because as a kid his head seemed as big as the Soviet satellite "Sputnik," hence *Spud.*

James (Fly) Williams. *Fly* because he would let the ball do just that, and with much success.

BOXING NAMES

While this chapter has focused so far on baseball, football, and basketball, boxing has perhaps some of the most colorful names in the world of sports. Here are ten favorites that oddly enough are based on the fighters' hometowns:

Muhammad (The Louisville Lip) Ali
Max (The Livermore Larruper) Baer
Billy (The Pittsburgh Kid) Conn

The Three All-Time Best in Their Sport

Who is the all-time greatest in a particular sport is a constant debate that never gets settled. For example, who was the best baseball player of all time, or football player, or basketball player, or boxer? And so on. But nearly everyone agrees that the following three athletes were the all-time greatest in their respective sports.

Wayne (The Great One) Gretsky. The *Great One* for his superb hockey playing.

Edson Arantes (Pelé) do Nascimento. *Pelé* got his nickname because one-word names are big in Brazilian sports. According to this soccer star, "Edson is the normal person, but he has defects. One day he is going to be dead. But Pelé, he is never going to die. I have to deal with both, but I think the bigger responsibility is to Edson, because he was born first. I don't know why I became Pelé. Only God knows."

Jack (The Golden Bear) Nicklaus. The *Golden Bear* is the nickname of golf's greatest player due to his blond hair and broad build. He also attended Upper Arlington High School, whose sports teams are the Golden Bears, in the Columbus, Ohio, area.

Jack (The Manassa Mauler) Dempsey
Jake (The Bronx Bull) LaMotta
Rocky (The Brockton Blockbuster) Marciano
John L. (The Boston Strongboy) Sullivan
Joe (The Barbados Demon) Walcott
Jess (The Pottawatomie Giant) Williams

Willard

CORPORATE NAMES

■

Naming a corporation is a serious undertaking—and it can be very expensive. As you'll see below, the most expensive name change in the business world was when Standard Oil switched over to Exxon. Then there's the story about Smucker's, a name that most of us would have gladly changed at the drop of a hat, but JM Smucker Co. stuck with the family name and used it to its advantage. As you will discover in this chapter, while some names were actually chosen quite casually, in most instances, corporations have made a big deal about selecting their names.

American Telephone & Telegraph Company (AT&T). Alexander Graham Bell invented the telephone in 1876. Only one year later his financial backers organized Bell Telephone and then New England Telephone. In 1879, with the help of Boston financiers, the two companies were consolidated as National Bell Telephone. When Bell's patent expired in the 1890s, hordes of independent phone companies jumped into the market. Struggling to compete, National Bell Telephone changed its name to American Telephone and Telegraph and in 1899 moved its headquarters from Boston to New York, focusing primarily on buying out smaller companies.

Anheuser-Busch Companies, Inc. Anheuser-Busch, the largest brewer in the world, started as the Bavarian Brewery, founded in St. Louis by George Schneider in 1852. Since Eberhard Anheuser put up a modest loan to help the brewery during rough times, he became the reluctant owner only a few years later. He put his new son-in-law, Adolphus Busch, to work as a salesman for the brewery. After proving himself, Busch became president of the Bavarian Brewery. Adolphus Busch died in 1913, leaving his son August in charge of the brewery, which he renamed Anheuser-Busch in 1919. The brewery is now the largest in the world.

Apple Computer, Inc. When Steven Jobs and Stephen Wozniak started their computer company in 1976, they wanted a name that would reflect a new venture and a fresh, exciting company—a nontraditional name that didn't conjure up a picture of a typical electronics firm. During a brainstorming session just before a deadline for filing a company name, someone came up with the name *Apple*. It made good sense. Apples were a favorite fruit of Jobs, and an apple has an image that represents something healthy, fresh, natural, and simple. Since nobody in the room was able to come up with a better name, the new company was christened Apple Computer. Following through on this theme, Apple named its most popular computer MacIntosh. When Steve Jobs left the company in September, 1985, he founded a new corporation. Knowing that the entire business world was waiting to see what he would do, he named the new company Next.

Avon Products, Inc. Avon Products was originally called the California Perfume Company founded in 1886 by David McConnell. The name was changed to Avon in 1950 after the Avon River in England, because McConnell thought the area around his Suffern, New York, laboratory resembled the countryside of William Shakespeare's home,

Stratford-on-Avon. Incidentally, the first Avon lady was Mrs. P.F.E. Albee, of Winchester, New York, the wife of a U.S. Senator.

BMW. BMW is the abbreviation of the full title of the German firm: Bayerische Motoren Werke ("Bavarian Motor Works"). The company was originally called BFW, for Bayerische Flugzeug-werke ("Bavarian Aircraft Works"), when founded in Munich in 1916 as an aero engine maker, but switched to BMW in the late 1920s.

BankAmerica Corporation. Amadeo Giannini founded the Bank of Italy in San Francisco in 1904. By 1921 he acquired the Bank of America of Los Angeles, which had 21 branches. By 1930 both banks were operating as Bank of America. The bank became the subsidiary of BankAmerica Corporation, a bank holding company formed in 1968.

H & R Block, Inc. Founded by Henry and Richard Bloch in 1954, H & R Block is the largest income tax preparation and electronic financing company in the world. It has 4,837 franchised outlets and 3,994 company-owned offices. Henry believed that because the company was a service business, it should bear their name. The founders dropped the *h* from their last name and added a *k* to avoid mispronunciations.

Borden, Inc. In the mid-nineteenth century, Gail Borden, Jr., invented the process to make milk nonperishable. His technique required condensation in a vacuum to preserve the milk. In 1856 he got a patent for his invention and a year later he established Gail Borden Jr., and Company. Borden got his break during the Civil War, when the U.S. Army placed an order for 500 pounds of condensed milk. Borden is now the nation's largest dairy company, the world's largest pasta producer, and the second-largest maker of salted snacks in North America.

Chiquita Brands International, Inc. Chiquita Brands International originated in 1870 when Lorenzo Baker brought 160 bunches of Jamaican bananas to New York City. Realizing his fruit was profitable, he and Andrew Preston, a Boston produce agent, formed the Boston Fruit Company in 1885. Four years later, the company merged with three other banana import companies and incorporated as United Fruit Company. In 1970, Eli Black bought United Fruit and changed its name to United Brands. In 1990 the company changed its name to the catchy, calypso-style Chiquita Brands International.

Chrysler Corporation. Chrysler Corporation was called the Maxwell Motor Car Company until 1925, two years after Walter Chrysler became company president. Chrysler is the smallest of the "Big Three" automakers (Chrysler, Ford, and GM). All other American automakers that have been established since Chrysler have failed.

Citicorp. Citicorp originated with the City Bank of New York. It was established in 1812 by Colonel Samuel Osgood, the first commissioner of the U.S. Treasury. The bank changed its name to National City Bank of New York during the Civil War. In 1955 it merged with First National to become First National City Bank. The bank formed a bank holding company in 1968 called First National City Corporation. It was renamed Citicorp in 1974.

The Coca-Cola Company. The company that markets what is now the world's best-known trademark, *Coca-Cola*, was founded in 1885 by Dr. John Styth Pemberton when he set up a chemical laboratory in Atlanta and went into the patent medicine business. Pemberton had previously invented such products as Indian Queen hair dye, Gingerine, and Tiplex liver pills. In 1886, he concocted a mixture of sugar, water, and extracts of the coca leaf and the kola nut. He added caffeine to the resulting syrup and marketed it for a while as a headache remedy. The name *Coca-Cola* is a combination of the product's two ingredients: coca leaf and kola nut. Pemberton changed *kola* to *cola* to go with coca.

Delta Air Lines, Inc. Delta was formed in Macon, Georgia, as the world's first crop-dusting service to combat the boll weevil that infested cotton fields in 1924. The company was renamed Delta Air Service in 1928 after the Mississippi Delta region served by the airline when it moved to Monroe, Louisiana. In 1929, Delta inaugurated passenger service between Dallas and Jackson, Mississippi. Shortly thereafter, routes to Atlanta and Charleston were added.

Equifax Inc. This huge Atlanta-based credit investigating company changed its name in 1975, after having been called Retail Credit Company. The change was made because its activities were far broader than its original focus in the retail industry.

Exxon Corporation. In 1972, after having been in business for 90 years, Standard Oil Company spent $100 million to change its name, making it the most expensive name change ever. More than 100 languages were studied, 7,000 interviews with consumers were conducted, and more than 15,000 telephone books were examined. Three years later, the huge oil company's name was changed to Exxon. Why Exxon? Linguistic consultants wanted a name that had no actual meaning in *any* language. Furthermore, it was easy to pronounce in most languages and it had no vulgar or objectionable meaning. They also sought a memorable word—the double *x* was thought to have a distinctive design.

The Gap, Inc. The Gap is a retail clothing store started in San Francisco in 1969 by Donald Fisher and his wife, Doris, who named the store after the "generation gap."

General Mills, Inc. General Mills was originally the Washburn-Crosby Company founded in 1866. In 1925, the company consolidated with other flour mills around the country under the name General Mills.

Gerber Products Company. Gerber Products Company started off as the Fremont Canning Company in Fremont, Michigan, established by Frank Gerber in 1901. His son Daniel discovered the need for a line of baby food after his wife asked him to strain food for the baby at the cannery; a practice parents had to do by hand at the time. By the end of 1928 the company released its first line of baby foods, and in 1941 the company changed its name to Gerber Products Company. Within two years the company dropped all of its adult foods. Now Gerber Products is the world's leading producer of processed baby foods.

The Gillette Company. King C. Gillette invented the idea of disposable razor blades in 1901 while shaving with a dull straight razor. After six years of trying to turn the idea into reality he joined MIT machinist William Nickerson and perfected the safety razor. They called their Boston company the American Safety Razor Company. In the early 1950s the name was changed to the Gillette Company.

Hallmark Cards, Inc. Hallmark cards have been around since 1910, when 18-year-old Joyce C. Hall started selling postcards from a rented room at the YMCA in Kansas City, Missouri. Only a few years later Joyce and his brother Rollie established Hall Brothers, a store specializing in stationery, gifts, and postcards. By the 1920s a third brother joined the firm and in 1954, the company changed its name to Hallmark. It went international three years later.

Holiday Inn, Worldwide. Kemmons Wilson founded Holiday Inn in 1952 when he opened a 120-room motel on the outskirts of Memphis, Tennessee. He based the name on a Bing Crosby–Danny Kaye film he had just seen, called *Holiday Inn.*

Honda Motor Company, Ltd. In 1946, Honda Technical Research Institute was established by Soichiro Honda in Hamamatsu, Shizuoka Prefecture in Japan. Two years later, the company incorporated and was renamed Honda Motor Company when it was capitalized at one million yen, or approximately $7,000. Today, it is one of the leading car companies in the world. Honda's U.S. marketing executives have expressed how thankful they are that Mr. Honda had an easily pronounceable name and one that English-speaking people could remember!

IBM. IBM's original name was the Computing-Tabulating-Recording Company. In its earliest days the company manufactured butcher scales and time clocks. In 1924 the name was changed to International Business Machines, usually referred to by the acronym IBM. The company has also been known as "Big Blue," a reference to its reputation on Wall Street as the "bluest of the blue chip" stocks. (The stock has since lost favor in the investment community.)

Kmart Corp. Named after its founder Sebastian S. Kresge, Kmart started off as Kresge variety stores in 1916. The name was changed to Kmart in 1977 after a board vote.

Land O'Lakes, Inc. Land O'Lakes was originally called the Minnesota Cooperative Creamery Association, which was founded in 1921. The current name was chosen by a contest in 1924. The winner won $500 in gold for the name "Land O'Lakes," based upon Minnesota's numerous lakes.

Lillian Vernon Corporation. In 1951 Lillian Hochberg created Lillian Vernon Corp., a mail order company for thrifty shoppers. Hochberg lived in Mount Vernon, N.Y., and combined her first name and the name of her Westchester County town when she founded the company. In 1990 she legally changed her name to Lillian Vernon.

McDonald's Corporation. In 1953, Roy Kroc, a salesman who sold a five-spindled milk shake machine called a Multimixer, called on a drive-in hamburger restaurant in San Bernardino, California, owned by two brothers, Dick and Mac McDonald. The restaurant did a booming business with sales totaling $350,000. Kroc was so impressed with the McDonald's operations that, at age 52, he convinced the McDonald brothers to give him the exclusive rights to franchise copies of their operation all over the United States. Through Kroc's efforts, McDonald's has since become a household word around the world. With more than 13,000 restaurants in 65 countries, McDonald's today is the world's largest food organization. The company serves 96 percent of American consumers each year and 7 percent of the U.S. population on a daily basis. It is the most popular eatery in the country, drawing more customers than its closest competitors, Burger King, Wendy's and Hardee's combined.

Mattel, Inc. Mattel was founded in 1945 by Harold Matson and Eliot Handler. They named their new company using letters from their first and last names, and started off selling toy furniture.

Navistar International Corp. International Harvester was founded in 1800 by Cyrus McCormick, the inventor of the mechanical reaper. In the early 1980s, the company's farm equipment business went deeply into the red and to save the company from bankruptcy, it was sold to Tenneco. What remained of International Harvester was its international truck and diesel engine operations. To shed its identity as a farm machinery company, the new management changed its name to *Navistar.*

Nike, Inc. Nike was originally named Blue Ribbon Sports by its founder, Phil Knight and Bill Bowerman. They changed the name to Nike in 1968 after the Greek goddess of victory, an appropriate name for a maker of running shoes. Founder and current CEO Phil Knight was a track star when attending the University of Oregon.

Pepsico., Inc. In 1898, Caleb D. Bradham, a drugstore manager in New Bern, North Carolina, developed a drink that was patterned after Coca-Cola but was intended to relieve indigestion. Since *cola* is not a registered trademark, he called his beverage Pepsi-Cola.

Ralston Purina Company. Originally called Robinson-Danforth Commission Company, in 1894 this firm's name was changed to Ralston Purina Company in 1902. The name *Purina* was taken from the company's slogan "Where purity is paramount," and *Ralston* from Everett Ralston, a well-known advocate of whole-grain foods who endorsed the company's products.

Reebok International Ltd. Headquartered in Boston, Reebok, one of the leaders in the sports shoe industry, was named in 1958 after a speedy African antelope.

Rockwell International Corporation. This giant manufacturing firm has had many name changes throughout the years. The Pittsburgh-based company originally manufactured water, gas, and parking meters under the name Rockwell Manufacturing Company. Its name was later changed to Rockwell Standard, and when it acquired North American Aviation in 1967, its name was changed to North American Rockwell Corporation. In 1973, the company became Rockwell International.

***Rolling Stone* Magazine.** *Rolling Stone* magazine was named after a famous Muddy Waters song, the same tune that inspired one of the world's most popular bands, The Rolling Stones. Jann Wenner founded the magazine in October, 1967, and ever since it has been published every two weeks and is now considered the bible of the popular music scene.

SAAB-Scania A.B. Founded in the early 1890s, the company was originally an English bicycle manufacturer with a factory in Malmo, Sweden, called the Svenska AB Humber & Company. The company manufactured automobiles, trucks, and buses, however, in 1929, it discontinued manufacturing cars. With the threat of war in Europe in the 1930s, Sweden realized that it was imperative to improve its defenses. With a need for a domestic aircraft industry to supply the Swedish forces with military aircraft, the Svenska Aeroplan Aktiebolaget, abbreviated SAAB, was formed in 1937. In 1947, SAAB reintroduced its new line of automobiles.

Samsonite Corporation. In 1910, company founder Jesse Shwayder chose the name *Samson* from the Bible. He wanted the quality of his luggage to be known for its strength.

Sara Lee Corporation. Consolidated Foods, founded in 1939, bought out Kitchens of Sara Lee in 1956. The baked goods company had been started in 1951 when Charles Lubin named his small food firm after his daughter, Sara. Consolidated is a conglomerate whose divisions sell such products as Hanes hosiery, Leggs stockings, Electrolux vacuum cleaners, Fuller brushes, and so on. In 1985 Consolidated Foods changed its name to Sara Lee Corporation. It was a bold move, and one against the trend of large companies that chose names based on projecting high-powered and aggressive images—a company couldn't choose a name more friendly and unpretentious than Sara Lee.

Sears Roebuck & Company. In 1886, at age 23, Richard Sears teamed up with Alvah Curtis Roebuck, a watchmaker, and the two men formed a catalog company in Chicago. In 1895, Roebuck sold his half interest to Julius Roenwald for $25,000. In 1908, Sears left the business and by 1913 he had sold all of his stock in the company. The giant catalog company didn't start opening retail stores until the 1920s. In 1993 the company ceased publishing its mail order catalogue, marking an end to more than a century of Sears Catalogues.

ServiceMaster. This multi-billion dollar cleaning and maintenance company with 5,500 franchises worldwide was incorporated in 1947 as Wade, Wenger and Associates. A few years later, its name was changed because, as founder Marion Wade said, "We wanted a name which could be applied to the diversified services we performed and at the same time indicate the basic philosophy of the company. . . . The word *ServiceMaster* struck us all as perfect in every area."

Shell Oil Company. Marcus Samuel named the Shell Oil Company after his first business, a novelty company specializing in sea shells. In the 1820s Samuel was importing fancy polished shells for his customers at the Shell Shop. Seeing a market for kerosene, he was soon importing it by the barrel. The company rapidly expanded and he renamed it the Shell Transport and Trading Company. It was thereafter called simply the Shell Oil Company.

Square D Company. The Square D Company began in 1902 as the McBride Manufacturing Company making electrical fuses in Detroit. The company got its name from the founders Bryson Horton and James McCarthy. The company changed its name to Detroit Fuse and Manufacturing and bought the rights to the Berry enclosed safety switch, an English invention. In 1915, Detroit Fuse introduced a new version of the switch and marketed it with a logo, a *D* in a square on the switch's cover. After much success with its new product, the company changed its name to Square D in 1917.

Subaru. Subaru cars were named for *Subaru*, which is the Japanese name for the Pleiades cluster of stars in the Taurus constellation. The cluster actually contains several hundred stars, but most people can only see the brightest six or seven. Subaru's symbol is these six stars.

US Air. US Air was originally called All American Aviation when incorporated in Delaware in 1937. The company changed its name to All American Airways after World War I, and then to Allegheny Airlines on January 2, 1953. After a major passenger survey in 1978, the company changed its name to US Air to change its image as a small, regional airline.

Volkswagen AG. Volkswagen was founded in 1937 in Wolfsburg, Germany. The company was the dream of two men,

Ferdinand Porsche and Adolf Hitler. Porsche, an engineer, had designed powerful luxury automobiles for Austro-Daimler, but had been dreaming of a small, low-priced car for the ordinary buyer since the early 1920s. Introduced in 1938, the roundish, odd-looking car became the basis of a plan to build an ideal worker's city. The name *Volkswagen* means "the people's car." During the late 1950s, Volkswagen was the number one selling foreign car in the United States.

A.B. Volvo. Volvo is a Latin word that means "I roll." Founded in 1915, and headquartered in Göteburg, Sweden, A.B. Volvo today is Scandinavia's largest industrial enterprise.

Xerox Corporation. Incorporated in 1906, Xerox was originally called the Haloid Company. The name was changed to Haloid Zerox in 1958 and then to *Xerox* in 1961. The name was based on a process of electrophotography called *Xerography,* from the ancient Greek words for "dry" and "writing."

Wendy's International. In 1969, Dave Thomas opened a hamburger restaurant in Columbus, Ohio, which he named after his eight-year-old daughter, Wendy. Wendy's real name was Melinda Lou, but her brothers and sisters couldn't pronounce it so they called her Wenda, then Wendy. There are more than 4,000 Wendy's restaurants today.

Wham-O Mfg. Co. Wham-O originated in the late 1940s when the founders of the company, Richard (Rich) Knerr and Arthur (Spud) Melin, started making and selling slingshots. They used the name Wham-O, the sound that a slingshot makes when you pull it back and let go. Wham-O went on to produce such products as the Hula Hoop, the Frisbee, and the Super Ball.

INTERESTING NAMES OF BUSINESSES

Business owners put in considerable time and effort coming up with clever names for their companies. They do it primarily because it's good for business. They figure people will think, Gosh, what an inventive person. Anyone that imaginative must have something good to offer. Also, an ingenious name is one that the public remembers. The following represents a cross-section of such exotic names of business establishments throughout America.

With a Name Like Smucker's

It sounds like something that was shouted at you after having stepped in front of a Manhattan cabbie during rush hour. *Smucker* is not the kind of last name you'd like to go through life with—that is, unless you happen to be part of the Smucker family that operates JM Smucker Co. in Orville, Ohio (headquarters are on Strawberry Lane).

JM Smucker, the well-known maker of jams and jellies, is a half-billion dollar business that knows how to make an asset out of what would normally appear to be a liability. It would have been logical to hire a Madison Avenue advertising agency to do an extensive search, followed by comprehensive surveys, and finally a name change combined with a full-scale ad campaign. But this is not Smucker's style. Instead, the company took a much different route by telling the world: "With a name like Smucker's, it has to be good." Holding the lion's share of the market, Smucker's strategy has worked exceedingly well.

THE RESTAURANT INDUSTRY

New York City
Bermuda Triangle
Hero to Eternity
Camp David
Recession Cafe

Miami
Your Father's Moustache
Sub Mission
The Yellow Submarine

San Diego
The Earthquake Cafe
Soup Exchange
Spice Rack

Washington, D.C.
Highbrows
Bull on the Beach
Frank N Stein
Pies on the Run
The Tombs
The Mad Hatter
Wok and Roll

Denver
The Denver Detour
Egg-Ception
The Loading Dock
Oinks Diner
Rock Bottom Brewery

Kansas City, Missouri
Franks A Lot
Wimp's Place
Wok of Fortune

Columbus, Ohio
Cheers Too

Minneapolis
The Egg and I
Franks A Million
Muddy Waters

Las Vegas
Loose Caboose
You Bet Your Buns

Philadelphia
Toastworks

Baltimore, Maryland
Judge's Bench
Something Fishy

Santa Fe, New Mexico
The Bull Ring
Legal Tender
The Mine Shaft

Atlanta
Eat Your Vegetables
Orchestra Pit
Wok and Roll

Cleveland
Chuck's Wagon
Everything and Then Some
The Milk Pail

San Francisco
Alcatraz
Chick and Coop

San Antonio
The Side Wok Cafe

Chicago
Doggie Dinner
Snacks Fifth Ave
Wiener Take All

Denver
Mustard's Last Stand

Orlando
Wok Inn

BAKERY NAMES

San Diego
The Dessert Cart
Flour Power

New York City
The Erotic Baker

Las Vegas
Cake Walk
Great Buns

Washington, D.C.
Sweet & Spicy

Minneapolis
A Toast to Bread
Flour Pot Cookie Shop
SuperMom's

Philadelphia
Rolling in Dough
Sweet Memories

Baltimore
Take the Cake

Santa Fe
Chocolate Maven

Atlanta
Pat-A-Cake
Piece of Cake

San Francisco
Blue Chip Cookies
Holey Bagel

Seattle
Strawberry Jam

Orlando
A Slice of Heaven
Your Just Desserts

BEAUTY AND BARBER SALONS

Los Angeles
The Hairtaker
The Broken Nail Crisis Center

Miami
The Hairport

New York City
Uppercut

Washington, D.C.
Great Lengths
Head West
The Clip Joint

Las Vegas
American Hair Force
Beauty and the Beast
The Chopping Block
Grooming Dales
Hair We Go

Denver
A Head of Our Time
Sit N Bull
Hair Brained Ideas

Washington, D.C.
Cut N'Dri
For Your Hair Only
Hot Heads
Who Cut Your Hair

Boston
Hair We Are
Hairs Looking at You, Kid
The Mane Event
Hair's What's Happening
Hairsay
Hairway to Heaven
It's Finally Hair

Atlanta
Cut It Out
Hairacy

Minneapolis
The Big Chair
Hair Force One

Columbus, Ohio
Hair I Am
Heads Turn Heads

227

St. Louis
The Bobby Pin
The Cutting Crew
A Head Start

Philadelphia
As You Like It
Beauty and the Beast

Baltimore
Head Hunters
Off the Top
Head to Toe

Santa Fe
Head Quarters

Atlanta
The Prime Cut
The Beauty Spot

Cleveland
Today's Headlines
The Curling Iron
Living Dolls

Dallas
Alter Ego
High Rollers

San Diego
Blazing Scissors

San Francisco
A Cut Above Castro

San Antonio
The Hair Line

Chicago
The Bald Spot
United Hair Lines
Wish You Were Hair

Denver
The Tortoise & The Hair

Tulsa
Cut Loose
Baldie's

Seattle
Cookie Cutter
Beauty and the Barber
It's a Hairloom
Ladies & Loggers
Split Endz

BOOKSTORES

Washington, D.C.
A Likely Story

Denver
The Bookies
The Bookworm
Tattered Cover
The Dusty Shelf

Washington D.C.
All Booked
Booked Up

Baltimore
Book Bag
Pages

Boston
Book Case
Murder Under Cover

Atlanta
Chapter One

Dallas
The Book Mark

Las Vegas
Read It Again Sam

San Francisco
Tall Tales

Minneapolis
Once Upon a Crime

Chicago
Drummer & Thumbs

St. Louis
Sober Camel

Seattle
Beauty and the Books

Philadelphia
Afterwords
Bump in the Night

RECORD SHOPS

New York City
All Ears
Earache
Rock's in Your Head

Minneapolis
Memory Lane

Boston
In Your Ear

Washington, D.C.
Sounds Reasonable
Flying Saucers

Atlanta
Criminal Records

Denver
Disky Business

Las Vegas
Spin Off Records

229

St. Louis
Now Hear This

Philadelphia
All Ears

Baltimore
Good Vibrations

San Francisco
The Vinyl Solution

Atlanta
Eat More Records

Cleveland
The Disco Den
The Music Box
Off the Record

Dallas
Direct Hit
Groves

Tulsa
Sounds Good to Me

FLOWER SHOPS

Columbus, Ohio
Lone Arranger & Pronto

Denver
Apricot Halves
Buds N' Blossoms

Minneapolis
Specialty Silks

Atlanta
Avant-Garden
The Briar Patch

Dallas
By Any Other Name

San Francisco
Cupid's Arrow
Under the Sun

MATERNITY SHOPS

Boston
A Pea in a Pod
From Here to Maternity

Brooklyn
The Coming Event
Future Mom

Denver
Before & After

Minneapolis
Maternal Instincts

Dallas
Daddy Did It
New Addition
Storkland

OPTICAL

Boston
For Eyes

Brooklyn
Clear Vision

Denver
I Care
New Vision
Peepers
The Visionary

Dallas
Agent Optical
Everything in Sight
Bye Bye Bifocals

Minneapolis
The Glasses Menagerie
Eyesight

ODDS AND ENDS

Bathing Suits
Alice's Undercover World, Los Angeles

Boots
Buffalo Chips Bootery, Manhattan

Wigs
Hair Today Gone Tomorrow, Denver

231

Dance Studio
New England Dinosaur, Manhattan

Day Care
Children's Underground, Manhattan

Pawn Shop
Mucho Money, Miami

Jewelry
Timely Innovations, New York City

Book Binders
Books Abound, Kansas City, Missouri

Pet Store
The Fishing Hole, Minneapolis
Purr-Fect Pets, Columbus, Ohio

Pet Grooming
Shear Delite, Columbus, Ohio

Rare Book Dealer
Book Ends, Boston

Candy Shop
Sweet N Counter, Milwaukee

Carry Out
Dial-A-Chicken, Atlanta

Pizza
Escape from New York, San Francisco
American Pie, Atlanta

Corporate Name Changes

In 1993, there were 1,285 corporate name changes in the United States. This compares to 1,069 in 1991, 1,321 in 1990, 1,600 in 1989, and 1,864 in 1988, which was a record year. Of the 1992 changes, 70 percent, or 899, were prompted by some strategic business activity, such as a merger, acquisition, spin-off, or reorganization. The number of companies voluntarily changing their names was 302, up from 221 in 1991. Perhaps the most significant name change in this category was Control Data, which opted for a distinctly new name, *Ceridian Corporation*, when it reshaped the company and spun off its computer business and the old name. Two of the most successful 1992 name changes to promote a corporate brand were *Snapple*, the bottled flavored beverage sold by Unadulterated Food Products and *Sprint*, the long-distance service that abandoned its former name, United Telecommunications. The reason for these changes is obvious: both Sprint and Snapple were more immediately recognizable than were the old names.

Caterers
Elbows & Appetites, Columbus, Ohio
Fringe Benefits, Columbus, Ohio
Made from Scratch Catering, Columbus, Ohio

Antique Shops
Buggy Whip Antiques, Columbus, Ohio
Down Memory Lane, Columbus, Ohio
Gilded Lily, Columbus, Ohio

Needlework Craft Stores
Cross My Heart, Columbus, Ohio
Double Cross, Columbus, Ohio

TRADEMARK NAMES

■

Trademark names are often valuable assets to companies. After all, it takes an enormous investment in money and time to become an established, recognized brand—and once this happens, it's prudent to protect that name. A registered trademark does just that. Under trademark law, anyone who uses a trademarked name without permission can be sued for infringement.

Trademark names protect company names as well as company products. The following list includes some well-known brand names of products and some trivia about them.

Adidas. Adidas sportswear was named in the 1920s after its German founder, Adolph (Adi) Dassler.

Alka-Seltzer. When Miles Laboratories introduced the antacid in 1931, the product was called Alka-Seltzer, because Alka is an abbreviation for "alkaline," the neutralizing ingredient used in this solution, and *seltzer* generally refers to fizzy water. The company first launched the product using the character named *Speedy*.

Aunt Jemima. In 1889 in St. Joseph, Missouri, Chris L. Rutt and two associates developed a self-rising pancake mix.

They decided a merchandising plan was needed for this new product. Rutt chose the name *Aunt Jemima* based on a vaudeville team of the same name. Not having the cash to promote the product, Rutt and his associates sold out to Davis Milling Company, whose growth skyrocketed after a huge promotion at the World's Columbian Exposition in Chicago in 1893. Nancy Green, a famed black cook from Kentucky, served pancakes at the exposition and her friendliness and warm personality were used to achieve much of the company's success.

Baby Ruth. Baby Ruth candy bars were named after President Grover Cleveland's eldest daughter, and not the famous baseball player, as many believe. The name was chosen by a contest sponsored by the Curtis Candy Company in the 1920s. When the company first introduced these nut bars they were called "Kandy Kake."

Betty Crocker. An enduring symbol of General Mills, Betty Crocker was created in 1921 as a marketing strategy directed at women. Executives at the Washburn-Crosby Flour Company, which later merged with other flour mills to form General Mills, anticipated that homemakers would trust the advice of a woman like themselves. The name *Betty* was chosen because it sounded friendly and reassuring, and *Crocker* was added in honor of a director of the company. Betty Crocker's look has been updated periodically, and continues to grace food packaging and cookbooks today.

Boeing. The Boeing line of jets was named after William Edward Boeing, who founded the company in 1916. The firm was originally called the Pacific Aero Products Company but was renamed the Boeing Airplane Company in 1917.

Trademark Dogs

Dogs are the most popular animals used as trademarks. The most recognized is RCA's Nipper, the lovable smooth hair fox terrier whose head is cocked to hear "His Master's Voice." Nipper was painted by his owner, Francis Barraud, in 1884 in Bristol, England, when he was seen sitting in front of the family gramophone. Barraud received 50 pounds sterling for his oil painting and another 50 pounds for the copyright. Recently, RCA has introduced the pint-sized terrier pup, in its commercials.

Tige, the Boston terrier, was created by Richard Fenton Outcault in 1902 and introduced at the St. Louis World's Fair by the Brown Shoe Company. He has been appearing with his master, Buster Brown ever since.

Other famous trademark dogs include the Dial Corporation's greyhound, adopted by the Greyhound Bus Line in the 1920s when a California passenger commented on his first bus ride, "It's as swift and graceful as a greyhound." Mack Trucks uses the bulldog, displayed as a hood ornament symbolizing toughness and dependability. Black and White Scotch uses a black Scottish terrier and a West Highland white terrier, and Hush Puppies has a basset hound.

Brillo. Brillo pads, introduced by Brillo Manufacturing Company in 1913, were named from the word *brilliant,* since they made cookware shine like new.

Budweiser Beer. Adolphus Busch named America's first national beer *Budweiser* in 1876. It was named after Budweis, in the former Czechoslovakia. The recipe was so popular that the ingredients and techniques of brewing of Budweiser are still the same. Budweiser is the world's best-selling beer and accounts for one out of every three beers sold in the United States.

■

Naming the Edsel

No other car manufactured has ever bombed like Ford's 1957 Edsel. More money was spent on its launching than on any other previous product offered to the public—a total of a quarter of a billion dollars was invested in what was to be the most perfectly conceived automobile ever introduced. The Ford Motor Company spent heavily in public opinion polls and in a new science called "motivational research." Of prime importance was the selection of a suitable name.

During its development, which started several years earlier, the car was referred to by Ford insiders as the "E" car, which stood for "experimental." Chairman Henry Ford II, his brothers and sister, and his mother, Eleanor Clay Ford, were determined that the car *not* be named Edsel after the late Edsel Ford, Henry's father. As he had expressed, the family "didn't want to see their father's name on thousands of spinning hubcaps."

In 1956 the company chose an advertising firm to come up with a name. A contest was held, netting 6,000 names. There was no consensus, however, among Ford executives, so the search continued. Marianne Moore, a well-known poet, submitted the following names: *the Ford Silver Sword, the Ford Faberge, Mongoose Civique, the Intelligent Whale, and Utopian Turtletop*, but they weren't accepted.

With cars about to come off the production line, time was running out and a name had to be chosen. Now desperate, a committee formed to select a name decided to go with *Edsel*. It was to serve as a lasting tribute to the memory of the son of the company's founder, and the father of its CEO. Deciding to go with the committee's recommendation, Henry II agreed with the choice as long as his family had no objections. When the other family members heard that Henry II had tentatively agreed to the name *Edsel*, they approved it, too. After all, Henry was the CEO.

When the Edsel was finally introduced in the showrooms on September 4, 1957, it was rejected by the public and only 11,000 were sold. The unattractive car quickly became the butt of many jokes and was given such nicknames as "pretzel," "weasel," "diesel," and "Edsel-smedsel." What was meant to be a tribute to a beloved member of the Ford family had become an embarrassment. Its main contribution is that in college business courses, it has become a classic example of what can go wrong. The word *Edsel* has become synonymous with a business *faux pas* of epic proportions.

Cadillac. The luxurious Cadillac, first manufactured in 1901 in Detroit, was named after the Frenchman Sieur de Cadillac, who founded Detroit in 1701.

Camel Cigarettes. Richard Joshua Reynolds, the founder of the J. R. Reynolds Tobacco Company, chose the name *Camel* for his new brand of cigarettes in the early 1900s because of the current fashion for exotic names. He chose Camel because of its association with the mysterious Orient and Turkish tobaccos.

Coke. The Coca-Cola Company adopted the name *Coke* for its now famous soft drink in 1920 because a rival firm, the Koke Company, produced a similar cola drink at that time. Coca-Cola adopted the name *Coke* to differentiate its product. Of course, it is now the most popular beverage in the world. Cola drinks are made with the nuts of the African cola tree.

Cutty Sark Scotch. This fine scotch was originally called *Berry Bros. Scotch Whiskey* since it was served by Berry's Coffee Mill in London, England. In the 1870s, the company decided to give it a more distinctive name. One of its patrons suggested *Cutty Sark* after the winner of a clipper ship race. Another patron, who happened to be an artist, sketched the ship and her name on a piece of yellow scratch paper. The sketch has been the label on the bottle, almost unchanged, ever since.

Trademark Names That Are *Not* Generic

These trademarked names are commonly thought to be generic, but are not.

Band-Aid. It was introduced in 1921 by Johnson & Johnson, though we tend to refer to all adhesive bandages by this name, Band-Aid is a trademark name.

Formica. Though *Formica* is often used to describe any plastic laminate, it is a trademark of the Formica Corporation.

Frigidaire. Although many people call their refrigerators a *Frigidaire*, it is still a trademark of the Frigidaire Company.

Jeep. Although many off-road and utility vehicles are called *Jeeps*, a Jeep is a registered trademark of the Chrysler Corporation.

Kleenex. Kleenex is a trademark registered with Kimberly-Clark, not just any tissue handkerchief.

Scotch Tape. Although many people ask for *Scotch Tape* when they want clear adhesive tape, Scotch Transparent Tape is manufactured only by the Minnesota Mining and Manufacturing Company.

Vaseline. This petroleum jelly product is a registered trademark of Cheseborough-Pond's.

Xerox. Though used commonly as both a noun and a verb to denote any photocopy, *Xerox* is a registered trademark of the Xerox Corporation.

Dom Perignon. Dom Perignon, a blind cellarmaster of the Benedictine monastery near Epernay, perfected the process of fermenting champagne in a bottle. His acute senses of taste and smell, developed by necessity, aided him in making and improving the wines. Moet et Chandon vineyards named its first vintage after him for his accomplishments.

Elsie the Cow. Elsie the Cow was originally an inanimate, advertising trademark used by the Borden Company to provide it with a friendly identity. But at the New York World's Fair in 1939, a live "Elsie" attracted 11,000,000 people to her colonial-style boudoir, complete with a four-poster bed. Elsie went on to become one of the most well-known symbols in the United States and in 1957 she bore twin calves, just in time to commemorate Borden's first 100 years.

Frisbee. The Frisbee was originally called the "Pluto Platter" flying disc when the founders of Wham-O Manufacturing Richard (Rich) Knerr and Arthur (Spud) Melin invented it in 1955. After many attempts to introduce the product under names like the "Wham-O Pluto Platter" and the "Sputnik," they decided to call it the Frisbee in 1961 after a famous cartoon character who would always say, "Don't be a Frisbee."

Hula Hoop. The Hula Hoop was introduced in the 1950s by Wham-O after a friend of the founders brought them a bamboo exercise hoop from India. Unknown to the general public, a similar hoop had been used by the American Indians as a toy. Wham-O sold 25 million Hula Hoops within four months, launching one of the biggest fads ever.

I.W. Harper. Isaac W. Bernheim came to New York from Germany in 1848 with only four dollars in his pocket. After many odd jobs Isaac became a bookkeeper for a wholesale

■

How Some Cars Were Named

Here's how some well-known cars were named:

Achieva. This Oldsmobile model has a computer-generated name, or neologism. It doesn't mean anything but it connotes achievement. Originally the car was called "Achiever," but it was changed to *Achieva* to remove the stigma of a young urban professional who had "made it."

Acura. This is another neologism that suggests precision. Name Lab worked with Honda Motor Company with the understanding that one of the company's desired associations for the brand was precise engineering.

Altima. This new word hints at *ultimate* or *best*, but doesn't have a real meaning. It replaced the Stanza, a name that never caught on.

Fairlane. This Ford model was named after company founder Henry Ford's estate, Fair Lane.

Geo. Chevrolet used a morpheme, the smallest meaningful language unit, to name this car, which is its smallest model. In many languages, *Geo* means "world."

Mitsubishi. This word means "three pebbles" in Japanese.

Mondeo. This new Ford "world car" was designed and engineered in North America and Europe for sale on both continents. In Italian, *Mondo* means "world."

Taurus. When the late Lew Veraldi, vice-president of Ford car product development, and John Risk, a top engineer, found out that both their wives were born under the Taurus sign of the zodiac, it was also a sign for naming the new model. Taurus was the project code name that eventually became the name of the car.

Windstar. This 1994 minivan, as the successor to the Aerostar, was named for a specific purpose. Ford wanted to keep the relationship to the Aerostar, but at the same time make it different enough to persuade buyers the company was releasing a new vehicle.

---

liquor firm in Kentucky. He soon saved enough money to bring his brother Bernard into the country to work with him. The two brothers purchased a barrel of whiskey and opened for business in the back of a wholesale grocery store. Harper, one of their best salesman, was so popular that his customers referred to the whiskey as "Mr. Harper's whiskey." In 1872, the Bernheim brothers named their choicest whiskey I.W. Harper after Isaac's initials and the surname of their number-one salesman.

Heinz 57. Henry Heinz, founder of H.J. Heinz, thought of the name *Heinz 57* in 1896 while riding a train in New York and seeing a brand of shoes offering "21 styles." He counted all the varieties of his firm's products and came up with the number 57.

Kodak. Inventor George Eastman chose the trademark name *Kodak* because, he said, "The letter *K* had been a favorite with me—it seemed a strong, incisive sort of letter. Therefore, the word I wanted had to start with *K*. Then it became a question of trying out a great number of combinations of letters that made words starting and ending with *K*. The word *Kodak* is the result. . . . It became the distinctive word for our products." Eastman founded the Eastman Kodak Company in the 1870s.

Suffering an Identity Crisis

International Communications Research conducted a survey of more than 1,000 people asking whether they thought of the following trademarked products as brand names made by a single company or as a generic product. Here are percentages of people who responded that the word referred to a generic product.

Band-Aid	61%	Q-Tips	48%
Kleenex	56%	Jell-O	42%
Scotch Tape	52%	Fritos	29%
Xerox	49%	Coke	29%

Levi's. Levi's blue jeans were named after the company's founder, Levi Strauss. He was a Bavarian immigrant who came to San Francisco from New York by ship in 1850, just after the big gold rush in 1849. He carried with him goods from his brother's clothing shop but sold all his merchandise during his trip with the exception of a roll of tent canvas. Strauss learned that the miners' pants often ripped and tore during strenuous work, so he fashioned a pair of pants from the canvas he brought with him. A miner bought them, and the first pair of Levi's was born. The idea caught on in the mining camps. Later Strauss started dying them blue and adding copper rivets.

Life Savers. In the early 1900s Clarence Crane, a small candy manufacturer in Cleveland, Ohio, named "the candy mint with a hole" Life Savers because of their breath-saving qualities.

Lincoln Continental Mark II. In 1955, the Ford Motor Company's first postwar Lincoln Continental was labeled *Mark*

II. This was the first use of the term *Mark* as applied to cars of American manufacture. British automakers such as the creators of the Jaguar had been using it for some time. The term stems from the military jargon of Hitler's *Wehrmacht,* which designated successive refinements of tank models as *Mark II, Mark III,* etc.

Maxwell House Coffee. Joel Cheek, a salesman for a wholesale grocery firm, traveled through Tennessee on horseback in the 1870s with his coffee blends. He discovered the perfect blend and took it to the Maxwell House, a distinguished hotel in Nashville that symbolized the finest in Southern hospitality. Joel's brew called "Maxwell House Coffee" quickly became a specialty at the hotel. In 1907, President Theodore Roosevelt is said to have had a cup of coffee and exclaimed, "That coffee is good to the last drop," hence a slogan was born.

Noxzema. In the early 1900s George Avery Bunting developed a skin care formula in the back of his drugstore. He originally called it "Dr. Bunting's Sunburn Remedy," but when a customer came in and said, "Doc, you know your sunburn cream sure knocked out my eczema," he changed the name to Noxzema Skin Cream. Noxzema is a brand name for Noxell Corp.

Phillips 66. Phillips Petroleum Company named its gasoline Phillips 66 in November 1927. A Phillips employee was testing a new fuel on a drive and said, "This car goes like sixty." "Sixty nothing," shouted the driver. "We're doing sixty-six." The test speed was mentioned the next day at a meeting to name the product. When asked where they had been driving, the employee replied, "Near Tulsa, on Highway 66." This coincidence was all that was needed to provide a name for the new fuel.

The Prudential Rock of Gibraltar. The company logo depicting the Rock of Gibraltar was developed in 1895 by Mortimer Remington, a young account executive of the J. Walter Thompson advertising agency in New York. Prudential was looking for a symbol for the company when, commuting to his office one day, Remington happened to notice the "Rock of Gibraltar," a large rock named after the famous Mediterranean peninsula, that juts upward from the Jersey meadows near the rail line. The symbol was adopted, standing for Prudential's solid dependability and the company devised the slogan, "own a piece of the rock."

7-Up. In 1929, when Charles Grigg started 7-Up in St. Louis, the company was called "Bib-label Lithiated Lemon-Lime Soda." Six names were considered and rejected before the company decided on a seventh, thus 7-Up was born. It was also packaged in a seven ounce bottle. It is believed the "Up" comes from a competitive product, "Bubbles Up."

Slinky. While working as a marine engineer in 1943 at the Cramp Ship Yard in Philadelphia, Richard James was sitting at his desk when a torsion spring fell off the shelf. It did not just fall off the shelf; instead, it "walked" across a row of books and bounced to the floor. As James later claimed, "I didn't invent the Slinky. It practically walked into my life!" Two years later, Richard and Betty James founded James Industries.

Super Ball. Wham-O Manufacturing introduced the Super Ball in 1965, naming it after its ability to bounce amazingly high. At the time, the word *super* was not yet in common use. The now-famous Super Bowl was called the NFL/AFL Championship Football Game and supposedly renamed "Super Bowl" after the Super Ball familiarized the word.

Tootsie Roll. Leo Hirshfield came from Austria to America in 1896 to sell his secret little chewy chocolate candy that he made in a roll form. His childhood sweetheart, whose name was Tootsie, was on his mind. Thus, the only name he could come up with for his chocolate candy was "Tootsie Roll."

White Horse Scotch Whiskey. White Horse Scotch Whiskey has been around since the fifteenth century when inns and taverns carried their own whiskey, usually named after the establishment. White Horse Scotch Whiskey was named after the famous White Horse Inn in the Cannongate, Edinburgh.

■

Trademark Names That Have Become Generic

Trademark laws insist that if you have a trademark, it's up to you to protect it, and you must stop others from using it. This means that if somebody else uses your trademark, and you don't notify the other party that he or she has infringed on your trademark, it becomes public domain. This means anyone can then use it. Many trademarked products have become generic in this way.

Sometimes companies do their jobs so well to create a public awareness for their trademark that everybody uses it as a common word to identify the product. Once a trademarked product becomes a generic word, the trademark is no longer valid. For example, when you have a headache, you simply ask for an aspirin; but at one time, it was a trademarked brand name of Bayer. As a result, Bayer does not have an exclusive right to use the word *aspirin* for its product.

The following products were at one time registered with the U.S. Patent and Trademark Office but are now referred to in everyday speech to describe an entire category of merchandise rather than a specific product of a manufacturer. Each of the following was intended to be exclusively used by its original owner but can now be used by anyone without penalty. These words have become "generic" just because they are descriptive of the product itself.

Aspirin. Astonishingly enough, the name of this pain reliever was once a trademark of Bayer. Originally, Bayer manufactured a product that was called *acetylsalicylic acid*, but it was too difficult for people to pronounce and remember. So in 1899 Bayer shortened the name to *Aspirin*. It caught on very well—so well in fact that it became generic through everyday use.

Cellophane. Cellophane was once a trademark of Du Pont de Nemours and Company but has become generic and can now be used by any manufacturer of this kind of wrapping paper. Du Pont itself began to use the coined name in describing wrapping paper, sometimes making reference to a class of cellulose products, not as a unique brand that it exclusively produced. When a competitor used the word *cellophane* to describe its product, Du Pont objected and took the company to court. Du Pont lost the case and thereby freed the word to enter the public domain. Today the word *cellophane* can be found in the dictionary defined as "a transparent substance made from cellulose, used as a wrapping to keep food, candy, tobacco, etc., fresh and clean."

Cornflakes. Cornflakes, once a brand name of Kellogg's, is now a generic term for any brand of this cereal, no matter who manufactures it.

Dry ice. Dry ice, a refrigerant, was once a registered trademark of Dry Ice Corp. but is now a generic term. Its scientific name is solidified carbon dioxide.

Escalator. The moving stairway known as an escalator was once used exclusively by the Otis Elevator Company, but it is no longer a trade name.

Linoleum. Linoleum was a trademark name of Armstrong Cork Co. that has become a generic word for this floor covering.

Mimeograph. This former trademarked brand of Dick Co., A.B. has also become a generic word for this copying process.

Murphy bed. The Murphy Door Bed Company, the original maker of Murphy Beds, saw its product become a common term because it did not protect the name as a trademark. Now, a bed that folds up into the closet is a murphy bed no matter who manufactures it.

Nylon. Nylon was once a registered trademark of Du Pont but has since become a generic word for this synthetic fiber.

Raisin bran. Raisin bran was once a registered trademark but has come to refer to any brand of this cereal.

Shredded wheat. This cereal was once a registered trademark of Nabisco, but today anyone can call this kind of cereal shredded wheat. Nabisco failed to protect its trademark and consequently shredded wheat became a common term.

Thermos. Thermos was once a trademark of the King-Seeley Thermos Company, but is now used to describe any type of vacuum flask that keeps food or liquid warm and cold.

Trampoline. Although trampoline was once a brand name, it is now used generically by all manufacturers to describe the tautly stretched, springy mount used for aerial aerobatics.

Yo-yo. Believe it or not, yo-yos were once a trademark of the Louis Marx and Co. when they were first on the market.

Zipper. This word was once a registered trademark of B. F. Goodrich but has since become a generic term for any of the interlocked fasteners.

Colorful Names on Wall Street

■

While the investment community has a reputation for being stuffy and strait-laced, you wouldn't know it from the colorful nicknames used throughout the industry. As you will find in this chapter, Wall Street wheelers and dealers have a language of their own. Unless you're privy to the lingo, there's not much chance you'll understand what they are saying when they congregate to talk shop. There's a lot of interesting lingo that doesn't make a whole lot of sense to outsiders. This chapter will help you decipher some of the more interesting Wall Street terms.

Aspirin Count Theory. A lighthearted market indicator that says the market will fall a year after aspirin production increases, and will rise a year later if aspirin production goes down.

Baby Bond. A convertible or straight-debt bond with a face value of less than $1,000 that brings the market within reach of small investors.

Back Door. A nickname for the U.S. Department of Treasury.

Bare Ass. Used to refer to the Boeing Company because the company's stock symbol is BA.

Bear. This term refers to a person who believes that commodity and/or stock prices will fall or slow down. The term dates to an eighteenth-century slang expression that was used on the London Exchange, "to sell a bear skin." Back then, a dealer would sell the skin before the bear was caught because he anticipated that the price would fall. A downward trend in prices is known as a bear market.

Bear Hug. A takeover offer. Corporate officers are caught in a bear hug when a takeover offer is good enough to entice some shareholders, but not attractive enough to make everybody happy.

Bear Squeeze. Institutions sometimes know bears have sold securities short before prices go up, resulting in a bear panic. High bid prices force the bears to cover their shorts and take losses.

Bear Trap. A stock price that drops, after which many people sell, causing the price to surge back up again.

Bed and Breakfast Transaction. A British term for selling a security at a profit at the close of the trading day, then buying it back in the morning after the price has dropped.

Big Mac. A nickname for New York City's Municipal Assistance Corporation.

Bigger Fool Theory. Investors buy a security because they believe they can sell it at a later date to someone less knowledgeable.

Big Six. The six largest accounting firms in the United States, listed alphabetically, are: Arthur Andersen & Co., Coopers and Lybrand, Deloitte Haskins & Sells, Ernest &

Whinney, KPMG Peat, Marwick Mitchell, and Price Water-house & Co.

Blue Chip. Nationally known common stock with a lengthy history of profit, growth, and quality management. IBM and Du Pont are examples of blue chip stocks. The name is a reference to poker chips and casino chips—the blue chips have higher values than chips of other colors.

Blue Sky Law. Securities must be registered according to the laws of each particular state before they can be sold in that state. Those stocks that do not follow a particular state's registration laws become restricted. The name came from a judge who once said a certain stock had as much value as a patch of blue sky.

Bobtail Pool. A group of investors involved in a speculative venture who have a common goal, but who act independently of each other.

Boiler Room. A room jammed with telephones where sales-people call long lists of prospective investors and try to sell them speculative or fraudulent securities.

Bull. This term refers to a person who believes that com-modity and/or stock prices will rise. While the term *Bear* is an old English term, *Bull* is strictly American. It was prob-ably invented to create a slang expression opposite from *Bear*—visually, a bull's horns point upward, hence an up-ward trend is called a bull market.

Casino Society. Investors who put their money into under-valued corporate assets, volatile futures contracts, or other speculative ventures in an effort to make fast money. It is a reference to a gambling casino.

Cats and Dogs. Speculative stocks with brief histories of sales, earnings, and dividend payment.

Cutting a Melon. Profits, either from securities or employee bonuses, are distributed by either cash or stock dividends.

Death Sentence. All utilities companies must be registered with the Securities and Exchange Commission, and no utility company can have more than three levels (i.e., the parent company, a subsidiary, and a sub-subsidiary). Any other existing affiliate or holding company must be dissolved.

Dog and Pony Show. A broker-dealer firm puts on a seminar to introduce a company's new product or service in order to attract the interest of its representatives.

Dummy. A person who acts on behalf of someone else in a business situation, but not on behalf of himself or herself. The dummy controls the other person's votes, but has no personal financial interest or ownership.

Eagle. A restricted and tightly controlled computer system at the New York Stock Exchange containing corporate information.

Fairy Godfather. A prospective supporter or investor in a particular company.

Fallen Angel. A well-known company's security with a value that dropped suddenly after a negative development or news report.

Fall Out of Bed. A market that suddenly drops lower than at any other recent time.

Fannie Mae. A nickname for the Federal National Mortgage Association, a government-sponsored corporation that buys and sells Farmers Home Administration and Veterans Administration mortgages, and some nongovernmentally backed mortgages.

Feeding the Ducks. An investor sells his or her stock as the stock's price is going up.

Fence Sitter. An investor who can't decide whether or not to invest in a particular venture.

Fireworks. A security's price shoots up quickly.

Fish. When one dealer tries to identify the buyer or seller working with another broker-dealer who is trying to trade a large block of securities.

Flower Bond. A Treasury bond that can be redeemed at par value when the owner dies so the proceeds can be used to pay any inheritance taxes.

Ginnie Mae. A nickname for the Government National Mortgage Association, which buys Veterans Administration and Federal Housing Administration mortgages, then issues bonds on pools of the mortgages. The bonds are commonly referred to as Ginnie Maes.

Gold Brick. A security that originally looks like a sound investment, but later turns out to be worthless.

Gold Bug. An analyst who is partial to gold investing, recommending to investors that gold is a safe place to put money because a depression or hyperinflation could push up its price.

Golden Handcuffs. A contract in which a broker agrees to stay with the same firm and receive profitable commissions and bonuses. Upon leaving the firm, the broker agrees to repay a portion of the money he or she earned while with the firm.

Golden Parachute. If a company is taken over, this provides the company's executive with profitable benefits (such as a large severance check and stock allowances). This ensures that the executive will be financially secure in the event of termination.

Granny Bond. A government savings bond available in England to retired citizens and citizens receiving money from the government.

Gray Knight. The second bidder in a corporate takeover attempt, who hopes to take advantage of any hostilities that may exist between the first bidder and the corporation. The corporation has not solicited this second party.

Greenmail. An investor buys a large block of stock with the intention of selling it to a corporate raider at a premium, or selling it back to the company at a higher premium to keep it out of the hands of the corporate raider.

Hiccup. A temporary market drop.

Humpty Dumpty Fund. A unit investment trust made up of shares of American Telephone and Telegraph and its regional companies (like Humpty Dumpty, the parent company has many pieces).

James Bond. Nickname for a U.S. Treasury bond that matures in the year 2007, so named because the maturity date is the agent number for James Bond, the fictitious character of books and films.

Junk Bond. A speculative bond with a rating of BB or lower from *Moody's* or *Standard & Poor*. Due to the high risk, these bonds are referred to as "Junk" versus "High Quality" investments.

Killer Bees. A team of specialists a corporation will hold on retainer to protect the company from a hostile takeover by using such tactics as issuing tender offers or holding proxy contests.

Knife. Nickname for the New York Futures Exchange, derived from the exchange's initials NYFE.

Lift a Leg. Closing one side of a straddle option position while leaving the other side open.

Lobster Trap. Used by companies with outstanding convertible securities to stop unfriendly takeovers. A lobster trap prevents a person who holds 10 percent or more of the company's voting shares from converting their holdings into common shares of stock. The system is so named after the real lobster traps, which net large lobsters while allowing smaller fish to escape through the net.

Loco. A term used to identify the place a commodity is being traded, derived from the word *location*.

Mooch. A person who wants to make big money fast, so he or she invests in securities without first investigating the market.

Mother Goose. A short, simple summary that explains a company's prospectus.

257

Nuclear War. When at least two companies compete with each other to take over a third company. The action is so named because it is usually destructive to all involved.

Pac-Man Defense. To avoid a hostile takeover or merger, the target company tries to buy control of the raider.

Plain Vanilla. A traditional, routine security offering with no special features.

Plato. A computer teaching and testing system, designed by the Control Data Corporation, for investment industry examinations.

Running in the Shorts. An investor buys a number of varied securities that are sold short in an effort to push the price up because doing so encourages the sellers to buy the securities back, which will push the prices up even further.

Sallie Mae. Nickname for the United States' Student Loan Marketing Association, which consists of securities based on a pool of student loans that financial institutions make to college students, guaranteed by the U.S. government's full faith and credit.

Sleeping Beauty. A takeover target that the raider has not yet approached.

Sunshine Law. A law that opens to the public government meetings, including those of the Securities and Exchange Commission and the Commodities Futures Trading Commission.

Sushi Bond. A Japanese bond denominated in Eurodollars.

Tin parachute. A plan that offers benefits to all employees who lose their jobs following a corporate takeover. This employee protection plan attempts to guarantee employees health and life insurance benefits, severance pay, and placement assistance.

Tom-Next. Tomorrow's business day to the next business day. A next business day settlement.

Ton. Nickname for $100 million.

Triple Witching Hour. The final hour of trading before equity, index options, and index futures contracts expire. Because of contract schedules, a triple witching hour will occur four times a year, each of which marks heavy trading.

Turkey. A security that has lost money for its investors.

Turtle-Blood. A stable security with low volatility and a price that is not expected to increase quickly.

Wallflower. A stock that no longer is popular with the investing public.

Wallpaper. A worthless securities certificate.

War Babies. Securities issued from companies involved in the defense industry.

White Elephant. An asset or property that costs more to maintain than it is worth, or an asset or investment that will definitely lose money.

White Knight. A party a company chooses to merge with in order to fend off an unwanted corporate raider.

White Squire. A risky management antitakeover maneuver in which the company places a large block of its shares into the hands of a friendly party whose financial interests are similar to those of the target company.

Yankees. American securities traded in Great Britain.

COMIC STRIP CHARACTERS

■

Entertainers and crooks aren't the only people to have aliases. Even comic strip and comic book characters have them. The following is an alphabetical list of comic strip heroes and their alter egos.

Comic Strip Character	Alter Ego
American Eagle	Jason Strongbow
Amphibion	Kingsley Rice
Batman	Bruce Wayne
Batspy	Bobolink Weemer
Batwoman	Kathy Kane
Blue Colt	Fred Parrish
Blue Devil	Dan Cassidy
The Blue Shield	Joseph Cartelli
The Blue Tracer	Bill Dunn
Captain America	Steve Rogers
Captain Comet	Adam Blake
Captain Marvel	Rick Jones
The Copperhead	Bob Wayne
Cosmic Boy	Rokk Krinn
Daredevil	Matthew Murdock
Doctor Spectrum	Joseph Ledger
Doctor Strange	Stephen Strange
The Fly	Thomas Troy

Fly-Man	Clip Foster
Forbush Man	Irving Forbush
Hawkeye	Clint Barton
The Hulk	Robert Bruce Banner
The Human Torch	Jonny Storm
The Invincible	Prince Amentep
Iceman	Bobby Drake
Invisible Woman	Susan Richards
Ironjaw	Roland
Iron Man	Anthony Stark
The Lone Ranger	John Reid
Mr. America	Tex Thomson
Mr. Fantastic	Reed Richards
The Peacemaker	Christopher Smith
Peregrine	Alain Racine
Phantasmo	Phil Anson
The Phantom	Kit Walker
Plastic Man	"Eel" O'Brien
Power Girl	Karen Starr
Power Man	Luke Cage
Power Princess	Zarda; Claire Debussy
Robin	Dick Grayson; Jason Todd; Tim Drake
Robotboy	Ape
Robotman	Cliff Steele
Rocketboy	Junior
Rocketeer	Cliff Secord
The Shade	Roger Brant
Sonik	William Parker
Son of Satan	Daimon Hellstrom
Son of Vulcan	Johnny Mann
Spider-Man	Peter Parker
Spider Widow	Dianne Grayton
Spider-Woman	Jessica Drew
Supergirl	Linda Lee Danvers
Super Goof	Goofy
Superman	Clark Kent

Super Teen	Betty Cooper
Superwoman	Kristen Wells
The Target	Niles Reed
Tarzan	John Clayton; Lord Greystoke
Texas Twister	Drew Daniels
The Thing	Benjamin Jacob Grimm
The Thin Man	Bruce Dickson
Thor	Donald Blake
Wolverine	Logan
Wonder Boy	Dick Cole
Wonder Girl	Donna Troy Long
Wonder Man	Simon Williams
Wonder Weed	William Wylie
Wonder Woman	Diana Prince

LI'L ABNER AND DICK TRACY

Two of the all-time, most popular comic characters were Chester Gould's *Dick Tracy* and Al Capp's *Li'l Abner*. Gould began his historic strip on October 12, 1931, and to this day the strip is widely circulated. Capp, whose real name was Alfred Gerald Caplan, began his daily strip on August 20, 1934, and it lasted until 1977.

Both Li'l Abner and Dick Tracy represent the kind of heroes America loves—heroes who are patriotic, honest, and always for the underdog. Still, the setting of the two strips couldn't have been more different. Li'l Abner, a strapping 6 foot, 3 inch hillbilly, roamed the hills of Kentucky in a fictitious rural area known as *Dogpatch*. Dick Tracy, an incorruptible policeman, hounded criminals in much the same way as real-life Eliot Ness in a large midwestern city, which had a strong resemblance to Chicago.

These two strips contain perhaps the most colorful names of comic characters ever to hit the press. The following are some of the more interesting from a cast of hundreds who have appeared during the past half century.

Dick Tracy Characters

Tracy's longtime, bumbling partner was *Pat Patton*, who eventually was promoted to chief of police, and his replacement was thereby introduced, *Sam Cathem*. Tracy's longtime girlfriend was *Tess Trueheart*, who eventually became Mrs. Tracy. *Junior Tracy* had a teenage sweetheart, *Popsie*.

B. O. Plenty and his wife, *Gravel Gertie*, are a down-and-out couple with hearts of gold. They are the parents of a beautiful daughter, *Sparkle Plenty*, who, after the character was created in 1947, became a best-selling doll.

Some of the most memorable characters include a host of file criminals such as:

Pruneface and his wife, *Mrs. Pruneface*, so named for their disfigured facial features. Their family pet rat is named *Mole*.

Laffy is a lock-jawed, unsightly man inflicted with rictus.

Flattop, a pug-nosed, fish-faced, flat-headed bad guy.

Little Face, a kingpin with an oversized head.

Wormy is so named for his blemished complexion.

Oodles, a grotesque and disgustingly obese man.

Flyface, a slovenly, dirty individual whose body odors are so repulsive that swarms of insects accompany him wherever he walks.

Rhodent, a loathsome, ratlike man who once asked his blind parents if they thought he was funny-looking.

Other bad guys whom the famed crimebuster chased throughout his exciting comic career are: *Itchy*, who constantly scratched himself; *Gargles*, a mouthwash racketeer; *The Brow*, a man without a forehead; *Mumbles*, a mumbling murderer; *Shakey*, who never stopped shaking; *Laffy*, a dope dealer with a hyena-like cackle; *Breathless Mahoney*, a trim, young blonde who was a cold-blooded killer; *Pear Shape*, a stout jewel thief; *Mr. Bribery*, who kept a wall-case collection of his enemies' shrunken heads; and his sinister sister, *Ugly Christine*, arguably his all-time, most wicked villainess, with looks so detestable that she wore her hair down to her chin and never showed her face.

Other characters include: *Mugg*, a huge, excitable boxer, and Tracy's faithful companion, whose proper name was *Barbel Von Nikelslit Dauber of Purple Woods*. *Frizletop*, a lovely lady who was also an amputee; *Acres O'Riley*, an enormously large woman, who was madly in love with *Heels Beals*, a tiny midget. *Diet Smith*, a bigger-than-life industrialist, who was always belching and clutching his oversized belly. Some space characters were even introduced in the 1960s and include *Moon Maid*, daughter of the *Governor of the Moon* (she later married *Junior Tracy* and bore him a daughter, *Honey Moon*).

Li'l Abner Characters

Li'l Abner was the main character in Al Capp's classic comic strip of the same name. He was the son of *Lucifer Ornamental "Pappy" Yokum* and *Pansy "Mammy" Yokum*, a pipe-smoking tiny lady and the matriarch of the *Yokum* family. Li'l Abner's longtime girlfriend was beautiful and innocent *Daisy Mae*, who later became *Mrs. Abner* (the lovable *Marryin' Sam* officiated the wedding ceremony).

Some of Abner's early adventures were encounters that took place in "New Yawk," where our hero visited his high-class aunt, a socialite named *Beatrixe, Duchess of Bopshire*. In

265

the Big Apple, characters included *Mimi van Pett,* a Park Avenue socialite; *Baron Slinkovitch of Skurvia,* and *Scaroff,* his lackey; *Mrs. Dolores Eppinham,* the arbitrator of etiquette; *Mary Anhn Astorbux,* an eight-year-old heiress who is the center of a scandalous custody battle; *Hattie Haggle,* New York's richest woman; *Sassy Sandra,* a marriageable nymphet; *Madame Mercedes Scorpio,* a gold-digging psychic; *Dr. Lopez,* a sinister man and his weird assistant, *Sanchez; Hip Tong,* the gang leader of the outlaw "House of Dragon;" *Mrs. Sneerworthy;* and *Gat Garson,* Abner's sinful double.

Still more well-known characters are the following: *Sir Cecil Cesspool* and his large-bosomed wife, *Lady Cesspool; Hairless Joe,* a hairy caveman and his Indian sidekick *Lonesome Polecat; General Bullmoose,* an industrialist ("What's good for General Bullmoose is good for the country"); *Available Jones; Stupefyin' Jones,* a shapely rival of *Daisy Mae; Moonbeam McSwine; Earthquake McGoon; Appassionata Von Climax;* and *Evil Eye Fleagle,* a bulging-eyed little man who could stop a moose in his tracks with his double whammy stare.

There was also a comic strip within the comic strip that featured a Dick Tracy-type character and Li'l Abner's hero, *Fearless Fosdick.* Fosdick's voracious sweetheart was *Prudence Pimpleton.* And, like Tracy, Fosdick's arch-enemies included such wretched and despicable villains as *Bombface, Banana-Face, Spinach Face,* and *Hamburger Face.*

On October 16, 1939, the mayor of Dogpatch proclaimed: "Whereas there be inside our town a passel of gals what ain't married but craves something awful to be. . . .we hereby proclaims and decrees. . . .Saturday, November 4th, *Sadie Hawkins Day,* whereupon a foot race will be held, the unmarried gals to chase the unmarried men and if they ketch them, the men by law must marry the gals and no two ways about it." Ever since, *Sadie Hawkins Day* has been a popular observance.

About the Author

Michael D. Shook, a recent graduate of Colorado State University, is now a full-time writer. He has written *The Book of Odds,* published by Penguin in 1991, and *It's About Time,* published in 1992, also by Penguin. He is also the author of a forthcoming book from Prentice Hall General Reference on legal trivia. Michael Shook stayed in Colorado after his schooling there, settling in Crested Butte.